The Computer Incident Response Planning Handbook

About the Author

N. K. McCarthy previously managed the Information Security Operations / Threat & Vulnerability Management for a Fortune 100 corporation for several years. His international staff performed round-the-clock security event monitoring and response. His responsibilities included security patch remediation, vulnerability scans and remediation, penetration testing, system configuration monitoring and remediation, maintaining various Computer Incident Response Plans (CIRPs), and managing an active threat portfolio for key business functions, users, application platforms, and persistent vulnerabilities.

With a career spanning more than 20 years in IT, Mr. McCarthy has held a wide range of roles including systems programming, IT consultant, technical management, and IT sales. He recently retired after 30-plus years as a Marine Corps reservist, obtaining the rank of Lieutenant Colonel. His last reserve assignment of five years was with the U.S. Cyber Command. After 9/11, Lt. Col. McCarthy was mobilized and spent almost four years on active duty as an Information Warfare Officer working at the U.S. Strategic Command, the Pentagon, and the National Security Agency (NSA). Mr. McCarthy also has 17 years of experience as a volunteer reserve police officer. In this capacity, he was able to attend U.S. DOJ (law enforcement only) training in computer forensics and advanced Internet investigations. He was also certified by FEMA for its Incident Command System (ICS) and the National Incident Management System (NIMS). Mr. McCarthy is currently on the board of directors of the San Francisco Bay Area and Silicon Valley chapter of the FBI's InfraGard program.

Mr. McCarthy has a B.S. degree in Computer Science, an M.B.A., and a CISSP. He is also the CEO of an SDVOB S-corporation with established and developing businesses in California and Nevada.

About the Contributors

Dr. Matthew Todd is the Chief Security Officer and Vice President of Risk and Technical Operations for Financial Engines (NASDAQ: FNGN), a financial advisor with more than $47 billion in assets under management. At Financial Engines, he is responsible for security, privacy, business continuity, audit, and risk management for the firm.

In addition to his work at Financial Engines, Dr. Todd is the president of the San Francisco Bay Area InfraGard chapter, representing more than 1000 volunteer InfraGard members. He has been a local mentor for the SANS Institute, is a CISM and CIPP, and holds the GSEC certification. He has more than 20 years of experience in the technology space and has been actively involved in information security for the last 15 years. He obtained his Ph.D. from Northwestern University and was a fellow of both the National Science Foundation (U.S.) and the Danish National Science Foundation.

Jeff Klaben is an Adjunct Professor with Santa Clara University's College of Engineering, where he currently teaches Information Assurance and Computer Forensics. He is also a principal with Neohapsis, helping Fortune 500 organizations and leading security technology providers overcome global challenges in technology risk management, competitive strategy, product engineering, compliance, and trusted collaboration to achieve break-through innovation. Previously, Jeff served as Group Director of Technology Risk Management at SanDisk, Chief Information Security Officer for Life Technologies, Engineering Group Director with Cadence Design Systems, and Senior Manager of Enterprise Architecture, IT Security, and Compliance at Applied Materials. He also led product management, professional services delivery, and start-up incubation at Accenture.

Jeff is a frequent speaker at industry conferences, and for the past decade, has served on the board of directors of the San Francisco Bay Area InfraGard, a 501 (c)(3) nonprofit and public/private partnership dedicated to information sharing for critical infrastructure protection. He assisted the White House as town hall moderator for the rollout of the National Strategy to Secure Cyberspace and was recognized by the U.S. Department of Justice with awards for Dedicated Service and Exceptional Service in the Public Interest. He also received the Belotti Award for Outstanding Business Policy in High Technology Firms from Santa Clara University's Leavey School of Business. Jeff earned an M.B.A. from Santa Clara University, a B.S. in Information Systems from Wright State University, and the credentials of Certified Information Systems Security Professional (CISSP), Certified Information Security Manager (CISM), and Certified Information Systems Auditor (CISA).

About the Technical Editor

Suzanne Widup holds a B.S. in Computer Information Systems and an M.S. in Information Assurance. She is the president and founder of the Digital Forensics Association and the author of "The Leaking Vault" data breach report series. She has significant experience in digital forensics, incident response, and eDiscovery in the corporate environment. Her background includes 16 years of security and UNIX system administration, database administration, and software development. Suzanne is currently pursuing a Ph.D. in Information Systems with a concentration in Information Security from Nova Southeastern University.

The Computer Incident Response Planning Handbook:

Executable Plans for Protecting Information at Risk

N. K. McCarthy

New York   Chicago   San Francisco
Lisbon   London   Madrid   Mexico City
Milan   New Delhi   San Juan
Seoul   Singapore   Sydney   Toronto

The *McGraw·Hill* Companies

Cataloging-in-Publication Data is on file with the Library of Congress

McGraw-Hill books are available at special quantity discounts to use as premiums and sales promotions, or for use in corporate training programs. To contact a representative, please e-mail us at bulksales@mcgraw-hill.com.

The Computer Incident Response Planning Handbook: Executable Plans for Protecting Information at Risk

1 2 3 4 5 6 7 8 9 0   DOC/DOC   1 0 9 8 7 6 5 4 3 2

ISBN   978-0-07-179039-0
MHID   0-07-179039-X

Sponsoring Editor Amy Jollymore
Editorial Supervisor Patty Mon
Project Manager Manisha Singh,
            Cenveo Publisher Services
Acquisitions Coordinator Ryan Willard
Technical Editor Suzanne Widup
Copy Editor Lisa Theobald

Proofreader Susie Elkind
Indexer Ted Laux
Production Supervisor Jean Bodeaux
Composition Cenveo Publisher Services
Illustration Cenveo Publisher Services
Art Director, Cover Jeff Weeks

Captain Mark D. Derickson USMC
9/19/63 – 3/29/92

Oh, how he missed his three "girls"
His job on the other side of the world
A sudden explosion, airborne catastrophe
A routine flight, this would not be
He did what every pilot was expected to do
Protecting the Marines that were his passengers and crew
But when they pulled that old frog from the Sea
They found his body where the pilot should be
His ultimate sacrifice, sad but true
Left her a widow raising two

They're both heroes to me
–NKM

THE SECRETARY OF THE NAVY
WASHINGTON

     The President of the United States takes pride in presenting the
DISTINGUISHED FLYING CROSS posthumously to

                    CAPTAIN MARK D. DERICKSON
                    UNITED STATES MARINE CORPS

for service as set forth in the following

CITATION:

     For extraordinary achievement while participating in aerial
flight as Aircraft Commander, Marine Medium Composite Helicopter
Squadron 166, 13th Marine Expeditionary Unit (Special Operations
Capable), I Marine Expeditionary Force, Fleet Marine Force, Pacific
on 29 March 1992. While conducting fastrope training, Captain
Derickson's SEA KNIGHT helicopter was wrecked by an in-flight
explosion and fire shortly after take-off. The aircraft quickly
lost power and began to plummet towards the water. With his cockpit
filled with dense black smoke and flames, he executed immediate
actions to ditch at-sea. Struggling valiantly to fly his dying
aircraft, Captain Derickson flawlessly controlled its descent and
successfully cushioned its impact with the water. In his last full
measure of devotion, he courageously remained at his controls to
hold the airframe upright to allow his crew and passengers more
time to escape as his helicopter sank beneath the waves. Captain
Derickson's unselfish sacrifice saved the lives of 14 fellow
Marines at the cost of his own life. By his superb airmanship,
personal bravery, and steadfast devotion to duty in the face of
hazardous flying conditions, Captain Derickson reflected great
credit upon himself and upheld the highest traditions of the Marine
Corps and the United States Naval Service.

                              For the President,

                              Secretary of the Navy

Contents

Acknowledgments

I would like to thank the following for their assistance with this book:

- ▶ Jeff Klaben and Matthew Todd: Your contributions to this book were invaluable. As past and current president(s) of the SF Bay Area/Silicon Valley InfraGard chapter, your volunteer efforts within the IT community are greatly appreciated.

- ▶ Amy Jollymore and Ryan Willard of McGraw-Hill: Thank you for helping me navigate this new world.

- ▶ Suzanne Widup: Thanks for the last-minute help.

- ▶ To my family: You all are the source of so much joy in my life.

Introduction

The Clock Is Ticking

As media reports abound with news of embarrassing data breaches and damaging cyber-attacks, cyber defenders seem to face a continually expanding threat landscape. There's certainly a degree of media hype, but beyond the hype, an unfortunate pattern is undeniable. Organizations are failing to respond effectively to many attacks.

Several factors are driving the unabated frequency of these failures. As information technology (IT) increasingly defines and interconnects our modern world, billions of "always-on" devices remain connected and potentially vulnerable to attack. Many new products and systems continue to be deployed with little regard to effective security controls. Traditional, opportunistic attack scenarios proliferate as amateur hackers are empowered by the sharing of user-friendly tools and methods. New business models blur trust boundaries and accountability for securing systems. Most significantly, the nature of cyber-threats is expanding into more sophisticated, complex, and focused attacks.

At an increasing rate, organized groups and governments appear to be investing significant resources in long-term patterns of attacks that focus on gathering intelligence from specific targets. This scenario, commonly referred to as an Advanced Persistent Threat (APT), includes a number of recent, highly publicized examples that we'll touch on here. Meanwhile, the clock keeps ticking toward inevitable news of yet another major exploit.

The Dire Consequences of Complexity

For the cyber defender, finding an effective approach to understand and protect a vast collection of vulnerable IT systems can be an ongoing struggle. Technologies such as virtualization, mobile devices, and cloud computing offer immense promise for organizations. Each enticing new technology also introduces additional complexity and potential for exploit or damage to an organization's existing systems and data. Some folks simply choose not to see or acknowledge these new threats. Others try to use abstract ideas like puffy clouds to make this complexity seem less daunting. The bottom line is that unprotected systems create opportunity for attack. Given enough time, the uninitiated learn that oversimplifying or ignoring real risks often comes at a very steep price.

For the cyber defender, these attacks become incidents when they involve an adversary who performs some action against a target with some type of undesirable results. Even if an organization's stakeholders do not yet fully realize or express it, they expect a plan to deal with these undesirable results. When a crisis strikes, this expectation can manifest in a very immediate and emotional way. Seasoned chief information security officers (CISOs) will attest that a damaging data breach or cyber-attack can be both a professional and a personal moment of truth. Organizations and cyber defenders who are caught unprepared may be forced to face their own set of very real and difficult emotions, such as confusion, desperation, regret, and despair.

This book offers a practical and immediately actionable alternative. We'll help you develop a plan for the most challenging circumstances—that is, what to do when things get out of control. Before we dive into the details of creating your plan, let's consider the bigger picture. Those tasked with protecting organizations from cyber-threats face three fundamental challenges: how to recognize and stay ahead of new threats, how to shape an organization's thinking to enable effective response, and ultimately how to respond when compromised.

Recognizing New Cyber-Threats

There's been a lot of chatter about cyber-security. Folks pay attention to the headlines when companies like T.J.Maxx experience data breaches that have a massive financial impact of many millions of dollars. Customers get annoyed when companies like Sony are breached and lose their PII (personally identifiable information). Companies like RSA worry when they are compromised and their customers' trust starts to waiver. Dozens of forward-thinking organizations like Google, Adobe, and Juniper Networks now publicly disclose instances when they are targeted by an ongoing cyber-attack. Even nations struggle to respond when other nations sponsor sophisticated cyber-espionage.

Examples of damaging data breaches and cyber-attacks will continually emerge. These headlines may be effective tools for elevating raw fear, but regurgitating scary stories can be otherwise pointless. To affect positive change, cyber defenders must create a more thoughtful, complete, and intelligent story about risk. Keep in mind that your stakeholders are not looking for a detailed rehashing of every major cyber-attack over the last decade. A more effective approach is to look beyond the minutiae and focus on the key elements of risk that are most relevant to an organization's stakeholders.

When educating others about threats, the main idea is to simplify by focusing on what they need to know to make effective decisions. Especially when making a case in favor of planning, avoid overkill. Our goal is to identify the significant patterns that might be relevant to incident response (IR) planning. To create some perspective on how known and emerging threats may impact an organization directly, a little historical context is helpful. The operative term here is a "little" context. This context can help you to

▶   recognize and categorize new threats

▶   plan and be better prepared to respond

▶   educate and assist others when they have questions or need help

Let's apply this new approach right now, by concisely deconstructing some of these sensational headlines to find a few constructive lessons for effective incident response planning.

Cyber-Espionage

"Titan Rain" is a code name for an ongoing program of cyber-espionage by China targeting sensitive data from the U.S. Department of Defense. The primary objective has been to gather information about systems that support critical U.S. infrastructure and defense capabilities. This program has persisted since 2002 and has included thousands of incidents and the successful collection of massive volumes of data. The focus of this and similar attacks has extended beyond U.S. government targets to include companies that work as government contractors. Companies such as Lockheed Martin, Boeing, Raytheon, Northrup Grumman, and Stratfor have experienced related data breaches. In some cases, losses included personal information of company employees. Some of these organizations may have been secondary targets, but being part of a supply chain or industry ecosystem can make an organization or individual a target for attack.

Information Wants to Be Free

WikiLeaks is an online organization that collects and publishes confidential and classified information provided by anonymous sources. WikiLeaks has released a considerable amount of otherwise secret information, both intentionally and inadvertently. There has been a great deal of public debate about the ethics and legality of these actions. For our purposes, we can steer clear of this debate.

Many information leaks are preventable, but even advanced data loss prevention tools are not fail-safe. Some stuff is going to get out when empowered individuals decide it needs to get out. Some are inspired by a cause, as advocates of the "information must be free" mantra or attempting to respond to a perceived injustice by shining the light of transparency. Regardless, this trend is not on the decline, and the next WikiLeaks event could be just around the corner.

Haktivist Malware with Motive

In 2010, e-mail messages with the subject line "Here you have" carried a sneaky little link. When unsuspecting individuals instinctively clicked the link, they unleashed a computer worm that automatically forwarded itself to the user's entire Windows Address Book. This attack quickly spread worldwide, but even unprepared organizations were able to clean this one up pretty quickly.

The unique spin here was that a hacker group known as the "Iraqi Resistance" claimed credit for this computer worm as a form of political protest. In a YouTube video, the group also stated that the virus wasn't as harmful as it could have been. There is an underlying, significant pattern here: the landscapes of real-world politics and cyber-threats are merging. Any notions that the virtual reality of cyberspace is insulated from the real world are now eroded.

Self-Justified Pretexting

This one is like an overused movie plot. Seemingly well-motivated insiders naively believe that they can keep their hands clean by leaving certain dirty details to others. An internal investigation at Hewlett-Packard involved private investigators who attempted to gather evidence by conducting illegal phone wiretaps and performing pretext calls. This pretexting was performed when the private investigators impersonated HP executives when calling phone companies and banks to collect confidential information. Bottom line: folks who don't believe the rules apply to them are a threat, and those who turn a blind eye are also at fault.

Lessons from an Avoidable Breach

An unfortunate lesson in inadequate incident response planning played out in the early months of 2011. A prominent consulting firm, HBGary, was hacked by a well-known hacker group called Anonymous. By using a stolen password, hackers gained unauthorized access to HBGary's e-mail service, which was built on a cloud-based service hosted by Google. An executive from HBGary quickly became aware of the hack and responded to the attack by shutting down the company's web site, but this action resulted in an unintended consequence.

When HBGary contacted Google to request that their e-mail service also be disabled, they encountered an unexpected obstacle. As they struggled to prevent unauthorized access to their e-mail, the only way the company could get Google to take action was to prove (authenticate) their true identity to Google. The method to authenticate their identity involved posting a unique file on the HBGary web site. With their web site down, their hands were tied and precious time to respond was lost.

In hindsight, this obstacle was avoidable. HBGary could have anticipated and then developed and tested a plan to respond to this type of incident. If they knew a default process would not work, they could have changed the process proactively. Without a tested plan, the company could not respond quickly enough to prevent hackers from downloading the company's confidential e-mail messages. The lesson: without an effective plan, HBGary suffered significant, long-term damage to its brand and customer trust.

Cyber-Crime, Guns for Hire, and Antiforensics

Cyber-crime has become an industry unto itself, and a very profitable one to boot. As a result, cyber-crime is not only commonplace, but growing. Cyber-criminals have found a lucrative business in identity theft and online fraud and are targeting organizations that handle data that could be useful for these purposes. They are using a new breed of coordinated attacks in pursuit of potentially profitable information such as credit card numbers, bank account information, and credentials to access other sites containing valuable information.

This presents two types of challenges for the cyber defender. The first is rather obvious: these adversaries are increasingly motivated by significant financial incentives. The second challenge is more disconcerting. Criminal enterprises are now competing quite effectively to hire top talent. Creative types with the right technical skills and "flexible" ethical standards are finding more and more opportunities to earn a healthy wage by applying their trade on the dark side.

Consider the case of the Kelihos botnet. This attack was sending 3.8 billion spam messages a day until it was taken down by Microsoft. The most relevant detail is about the creator and controller of Kelihos. A resident of St. Petersburg in the Russian Federation, Andrey N. Sabelnikov was a former employee of several anti-virus and computer security technology providers. His unique knowledge allowed him to construct viruses that included debug codes that enabled it to download and install the Kelihos agent onto vulnerable systems. Equally troubling is that some who are expert at analyzing cyber-attacks and their origins are also applying their skills to thwart and misdirect responders. Those skilled in the art of antiforensics apply methods to destroy evidence that may be useful to incident response and investigation.

A Persistent Data Breach

In 2009, Heartland Payment Systems disclosed that it was the target of a massive cyber-attack that resulted in one of the largest data breaches on record, including the estimated compromise of more than 130 million user accounts. Attackers were able to access the company's systems for nearly five months before they were detected. Targeted attacks can remain ongoing for months or years. Without the ability or intent to detect a breach, it is impossible to respond.

Advanced, Persistent Threats

Malware has been a key element in a number of targeted attacks. These attacks are often delivered through mechanisms such as malicious links in e-mails (spear-phishing) or in advertisements on web pages (aka malvertising). These methods were used in an attack known as Operation Aurora, which focused on gaining access inside major high-tech and security companies in order to steal valuable intellectual property and alter the source code used to build their software products and systems. Operation Aurora hit a number of companies such as Google, Intel, and Morgan Stanley. RSA (part of EMC) experienced a similar major breach when the integrity of systems supporting the company's SecurID product were partially compromised. The successful attack on the SecurID product, which is used as an authentication tool for more than 40 million users, opened the door to more attacks against other organizations. Specialized security firms like HBGary worked to identify the attackers, but even this firm has been vulnerable to attack (see above).

There are a few important lessons here. First, even the big guys with massive security program investments are not successfully containing all attacks. So prevention is not (and will never be) a complete strategy for even the best-funded security program. The second lesson is especially disturbing. Core elements of your security infrastructure (and the infrastructure of third parties that you may trust and rely on) are now under attack. To maintain confidence in these systems, the controls that you would like to trust the most must be second-guessed and may need to be scrutinized in greater detail.

Adapting to a New Generation of Threats

With the growth of advanced, persistent attack methods, the cyber defender must adapt by preparing to piece together details from multiple exploits to mount an effective response. The Stuxnet attack is an ideal example of a sophisticated cyber-attack with a sophisticated objective. In 2010, this complex attack demonstrated how several threats could be combined to overcome multiple layers of security. It is commonly believed that the ultimate objective of Stuxnet was to disrupt programmable controllers used in Iran's nuclear enrichment processing facility, in order to setback the country's entire nuclear program. Stuxnet appears to have involved a serious investment of effort and brainpower.

The attack first inserted malware (a computer virus) onto the internal network of its target. This may have been accomplished intentionally or inadvertently by an organizational insider. It may have been installed directly on a PC or server, transferred from an infected USB storage device, sent as a link in a targeted e-mail (aka spear-fishing), or somehow spread through methods using social engineering (that is, availing itself using information gathered from social networking tools). In any case, the malware successfully installed itself on a system inside the organization's network firewall without detection. Stuxnet then used several zero-day vulnerabilities to gain control over an internal Windows computer system. At the time, these zero-day vulnerabilities were not commonly known and did not have security patches available to system administrators to plug the holes. These zero-day vulnerabilities may have been uniquely engineered for this attack, so it may have been quite difficult to detect, let alone correct the particular security holes that were exploited.

While avoiding detection, the attack then combined a number of methods to gain access to processes on trusted internal systems. When the Stuxnet software became fully operational, it collected information about internal systems and then initiated contact with external "command and control servers." This may have allowed Stuxnet to update itself with additional instructions on how to proceed with the attack. The attack then spread by infecting other internal systems using a combination of methods. The infection continued to spread on internal systems in an effort to find Windows systems running network control software from Siemens. When found, Stuxnet exploited a hardcoded password used in the Siemens software. Stuxnet then used the Siemens software to find the system controllers that were its ultimate target. Additional methods were used to take control of these programmable controllers and change how they operated in ways that advanced the underlying goal of the attack.

Lessons about how this attack might have been prevented are worth consideration, but they do not fall within the scope of this book. Let's stick to detection and response. In this case, the target appears to have been programmable controllers used in a nuclear processing facility. This is not especially significant. What is significant is that an attack was crafted with great precision with a specific target in mind. As in the HBGary incident, several obstacles hindered an effective response to this attack.

Ideally, the target would have anticipated and then developed and tested a plan to respond to this type of incident. Even without complete foresight, proactive vulnerability assessments could have helped to detect that an attack was underway. Further, the process of planning and testing could have highlighted a handful of vulnerabilities that may have led to some proactive, short-term improvements. This is worth repeating: The process of planning and testing alone could have highlighted vulnerabilities and led to some proactive, short-term improvements that might have limited the severity of damage from this attack. Without a tested plan, the organization could not effectively detect or respond quickly enough to prevent attackers from achieving their goals. The result was significant damage with long-term impact.

Shaping an Organization's Thinking to Enable Effective Response

Emotion is an expensive luxury during a crisis. Without focus and logic to drive decisions, precious time can be lost. An inclusive approach to planning for incident response can allow an organization to forget fear and just focus on being prepared.

Beyond just being prepared to deal with bad news, the trick to creating a really effective IR program is helping to foster a corporate climate where folks want to know the bad news.

The Primary Objective: Creating Advantage

Like a lot of things, advantage is the name of the game in incident response planning. To understand and survive in the natural world, the world of business, or cyberspace, consider how folks struggle to find a position of advantage. Advantage can be created by knowing what is desired, creating circumstances that improve chances for success, and moving to seize unique opportunities.

Creating a sustainable competitive advantage is the foundation of effective business strategy. Individuals and organizations continually attempt to stack the deck in their favor—with varying standards for ethical behavior. In the hacker culture, advantage can mean demonstrating superior abilities to think (or code) outside the box. Similarly, criminal enterprises find ways to sustain advantage by sidestepping or disregarding the laws that constrain others. It gets really interesting when the worlds of business, criminal enterprise, and hacker culture intersect. As IT proliferates in each of these domains, these intersections are happening with greater frequency, and in many cases with greater fallout.

Enterprises are in business to take risks and reap the potential rewards. Smart organizations understand that these risks include the possibility of data breach or cyber-attack. However, some choose to look at these breaches as though they were natural disasters—unplanned events that are impossible to foresee. Others fall into the trap of adaptive expectations about risk—that is, they can get stuck believing that their past experience with cyber-attack or data breach are a good predictor of the future. Failure to understand the potential implications or probability of these risks will seriously hinder response planning efforts.

In contrast, really smart organizations learn to overcome this fallacy by creating predictive expectations about risk. They view these breaches as events with some calculable probability. Knowing whether or not an attack had malicious intent may be less important than understanding the vulnerability that's exploited by the attack. In many cases, the probability of a damaging security breach has a strong positive correlation with both the deployment of vulnerable systems and the advent of new vulnerabilities that can touch these systems. Potential outcomes can include damage to the organization's reputation, legal liability, regulatory compliance findings, and financial losses that could jeopardize an organization's future.

In some cases, it is hard to fault an organization for failing to respond effectively to a new, unpredictable threat. However, these cases are quite rare. The new reality is that targets have openly expanded beyond "every organization that may have valuable assets worth taking" to "every organization that can be publicly embarrassed to make a point." In most cases, effective planning can reduce both the potential for an attack and scope of damage if or when a breach occurs. In essence, your plan will help your organization create or maintain a competitive advantage when things turn sideways.

A New Approach: Simplifying the Technology Challenge

One of the most pressing demands on an information security leader is to be prepared to deliver while under pressure. During an incident, the cyber defender can have more things coming at him or her faster, and with a need for quicker response than at any other time. The challenge of creating and maintaining an incident response plan expands as business models and supporting IT environments grow more complex. Some leaders try to address this demand proactively by transferring responsibility to a third party or implementing a new security technology.

Paradoxically, third parties and new solutions can just add complexity, which serves to expand the problem. The ultimate challenge for many information security leaders is in managing complexity. The trick is to find and keep what works and cut away the rest. Simplification is one of the information security manager's best weapons to combat an array of evolving threats. Better approaches are simplified by design and proven in the real world. A battle-hardened plan gets the security manager one step closer to being in a position to take action when required.

This book attempts to distinguish itself by providing a foundation based on a real-world tested, streamlined, and simplified incident response plan. When coupled with meaningful data points on emerging threats, an organization can position itself with a powerful capability to respond.

Dealing with "Bad" News

The world is chock-full of people and organizations who actively try to avoid bad news. These individuals and organizations eventually fail. Choosing to behave like an ostrich with its head in the sand is akin to enabling bad things to happen. No CISO or security manager worth their salt can expect to take a passive approach to finding vulnerabilities and expect to keep their job in the long run. As a CISO, I have taken a firm stand that I cannot do my job without basic knowledge of my organization's infrastructure and vulnerabilities. If we break something (which we have) during a vulnerability assessment or incident response test, I still expect stakeholders to thank me and reassure me that they will fix the issue promptly (with my help as appropriate).

James Morgan, our former CEO at Applied Materials (a Fortune 500 semiconductor technology company), had a most excellent mantra: "Good news is no news, no news is bad news, and bad news is good news." By seeking and proactively addressing bad news, Applied Materials developed a winning corporate culture of creating "good news." This proactive management philosophy has served the company well for decades. It's a smart way to run a business, and it's also a smart way to tackle incident response planning.

Postponing vulnerability assessments or incident response planning is a conscious decision for inaction. This is a decision that may need to be explained to auditors or stakeholders at some point in the future. The sooner an organization understands their real problems, the sooner they can start to fix them. This is a much better story to tell if or when something goes wrong and may significantly reduce liability or negative perception in the event of a breach.

Breaking Through Inertia

Some organizations don't fully recognize the importance of incident response planning until disaster strikes. In these cases, an information security leader has a responsibility to make this need felt (in ethically sound ways) and help the organization to invest and prepare itself for scenarios that represent high risk. As an advisor to a number of major organizations, I counsel industry leaders on cyber-security strategy.

For some, the first steps in taking a proactive approach to cyber-security are the most difficult. For example, some organizations are reluctant to start planning for incident response or to perform even cursory network scans or vulnerability assessments to understand their current exposure. They debate whether performing a scan is a good idea or if it might be a safer bet to do nothing. Fear to take action is useful information in itself. It could imply that an individual

► has not socialized or gained buy-in from other stakeholders in the organization

► does not have the authority or impunity to initiate unannounced security assessments

► does not have sufficient "cover" from senior management and, as a result, taking action could be a career-limiting decision (especially if this could highlight the inaction of others)

► does not feel prepared to respond if an unplanned event occurs

Those who prefer to do nothing often believe a passive approach reduces the chances that a vulnerable system will accidentally break or that they are in a more defensible position if they remain unaware of details about risks. This naïve mindset is based more on emotion than logic or technical facts. One thing is sure: those with a "do-nothing" mindset are likely to perpetuate an attitude that will ultimately damage the organization.

Inspiring Constructive Action

The trick to helping an organization overcome a "do-nothing" mindset is leading them to the right types of emotions that will drive them to take the right types of actions. Refocused, their fear will drive their decision to move forward with assessments and planning, perhaps with a greater sense of urgency. It's not about convincing anyone that nothing bad can happen during an assessment or test; it's about convincing them that even with a small chance that something could go wrong, the exercise is still worth the risk. If something gets knocked over easily by an unobtrusive scan or response planning exercise, it is no longer a low likelihood threat. They need to see that taking action is a safer and better choice than inaction, especially when this action allows control over timing and scope.

Responding Without a Plan

Nothing will replace planning and testing. The rest of this book will help you create an effective plan for incident response. The bottom line is that there are no effective substitutes for a well-thought-through, documented, tested, and actionable plan. Many stakeholders believe (or will believe) it is inexcusable to remain unprepared. The new reality is that a well-maintained incident response plan has become part of the baseline for a "reasonable" information security program. Beyond this, an effective incident response program requires more than containment of stand-alone incidents. Stakeholders expect organizations to 1) proactively establish a practical and effective incident response capability and 2) continue to evolve security controls to maintain a reasonable level of due diligence.

Why This Book?

Organized criminal attacks, sophisticated malware infections, insider threats, or just simply complying with all your various statutory and contractual obligations—organizations today, ranging from the board of directors, all the way down to that Information Security first responder, have a much higher burden of due diligence than ever before. *The Computer Incident Response Planning Handbook* is the only book that provides both the background knowledge of *why* and the step-by-step process of *how* to develop thorough actionable incident response plans to address the wide range of issues organizations face in time of crisis.

Who Should Read This Book

Starting at the highest levels of corporations, boards of directors are now being held responsible for their organizations' due diligence in protecting the personal data of the organization's customers and employees. These obligations are filtering down through the various layers of the organization (CIO, directors, managers) until they reach that InfoSec manger or analyst who is directed to develop and maintain CIRPs. These efforts are ultimately audited against standards like SOX and PCI and are the best way to manage requirements mandated by federal statutes such as HIPAA, FTC, and SEC. Numerous states have also enacted legislation much like California's SB-1386/SB-24 data breach notification law that places additional obligations on organizations.

This book is not a technical book. The knowledge gained by this book can also be applied to other corporate risks and assist in preparing for times of any crisis.

This book will also be of interest to non-IT readers who are interested in what is happening "in the trenches" as organizations struggle to protect *their* private information.

What This Book Covers

Computer incident response originally started in the technical depths of IT. Built largely around technical forensics and the intricacies of the different technology platforms, these efforts rarely strayed from the boundaries of IT. But with statutory, contractual, criminal, litigation, and brand impacts looming, more and more organizations have to expand their views about computer incident response planning and, for that matter, *corporate* crisis response planning.

This book will initially review current cyber-threats, provide an overview of how planning supports numerous organizations, and review at a high level the nature of crisis. Unlike many of the books currently available, this book is derived from actual plans in place—plans that have survived various audits and the rigors of repeated execution and that continue to provide recognizable benefits to their organizations. The book will then discuss in detail two real-world plans: a PCI-centric data breach and a malware outbreak. At the completion of this book, you will have the ability to produce actionable plans. This effort will also provide you with valuable insights into developing actionable plans for other non-computer risks.

How to Use This Book

This book is *not* intended to be a text book. Our hope is that the narrative tone of the book will entice you to read the book through the various chapters. The book provides the reader some initial context about the threat environment, planning, crisis, industry due diligence, and some additional benefits that can come from developing a CIRP. We then spend a good portion of the book reviewing two actual real-world plans: PCI data breach and malware outbreak. These plans will be included in the book with a distinctive layout. The reader could in theory simply copy these plans, replace their names, and they would have a unique plan. We don't recommend that the reader do that, however. The book includes an appendix and a glossary to assist you.

How This Book Is Organized

The book starts off at a "6000-foot level" to provide the reader some initial context. We start by introducing the reader to some of the latest cyber-threats. The second section of the book discusses planning, crisis, industry due diligence, and some additional benefits that can come from developing a CIRP. We then drill a little deeper into some theory and ideas about actually developing your plan(s). The main content of the book will then spend six chapters reviewing two actual real-world plans: PCI data breach and malware outbreak. These plans are highlighted with a unique layout. The book then concludes with some final thoughts.

The Threat Landscape

CHAPTER

1

Introduction to
Planning and Crisis

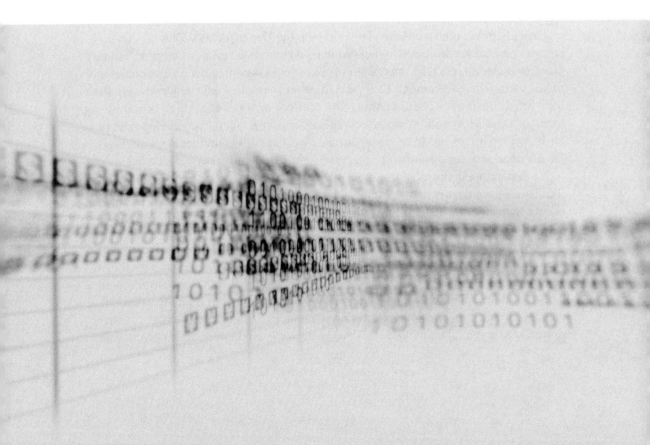

One of the first pages you will see in all of my Computer Incident Response Plans (CIRP) is a foreword. The first line on the page is "A Plan Is Preparation Manifested."

The word "plan" can be either a verb or a noun. We plan for retirement or plan the wedding of a son or daughter. We make dinner plans—a noun here. And we also create incident response plans, business plans, disaster recovery plans, and business continuity plans.

I've spent a fair amount of time associated with the military, and many of my comments here are based upon that experience. The military has a whole world of planning that is largely unknown to the masses. There are people who plan for the most dreadful things that you can imagine.

For example, as I write, I'm looking at the *Contra Costa Times* newspaper of Sunday, October 10, 2010; the title of the article is "U.S. Weighed Nuclear Options for Decades: Newly released files show plans against secretive regime [North Korea] in place for years." This demonstrates the fact that even if one has a plan in place, this does not necessarily mean one is going to use it. But it does mean that at some point, the government viewed this risk as a crisis waiting to happen. To be unprepared for this risk would have been unacceptable. What would have been newsworthy in my opinion, is if the U.S. government did *not* have any plans for a nuclear confrontation with North Korea.

The U.S. government and, to a larger extent, the Department of Defense have entire organizations dedicated to the idea that you plan in an effort to prepare. Military planning, however, isn't the only planning that's underway in hallways and conference rooms within the government. Every day, new and seasoned entrepreneurs visit their local Small Business Administration (SBA) offices in hopes of starting or improving their business. Most will ultimately complete a business plan. The development of a business plan forces one to try to be as objective as possible to document all those factors necessary for the creation, execution, and ultimate success of a business.

It's in developing that plan that the SBA volunteers start asking questions that many idealistic entrepreneurs may not have considered or simply overlooked—questions about competition, the defensibility of the business, regulations, financing, and taxation. These are necessary questions that must be answered and often aren't considered by the entrepreneur with the next great technology or service offering. Business plans are valuable not only to help the entrepreneur better understand the business they're getting into, but also to socialize this idea with the many different people who will be part of developing or supporting this new business. Whether it be the banker or venture capitalist for financing, third-party resources and partners such as suppliers or resellers, potential employees, or key executives—all these various players want to know what you're doing and, more importantly, is it worth their time and energies to support your new business initiative.

The problem with planning, however, is that although you strive to cover all the possible issues, your plans don't necessarily answer all the questions. Since it's impossible to forecast the future, sometimes the answers you developed for your plan aren't the right ones.

The military has a common saying around planning: "No plan survives first contact with the enemy." Although I totally believe in that statement, I also believe you *must* go through the effort of developing a plan. But when everything is said and done, it's the "execution" of the plan and not the plan itself that matters most. Planning is the "manifestation of preparation" for that moment when that new business will face the challenges of customers and competition, or when the organization will respond to a risk that has now emerged and has the potential to become a crisis.

The Absence of Planning

So far in this chapter we've discussed this idea of planning and preparation. I would like to spend the next few moments discussing an instance in which there was a crisis for which there was no planning.

In the fall of 2008, Conficker was probably one of the most prolific viruses to hit the Internet. Imagine for a second a Fortune 100 organization that did not have an incident response plan for a virus outbreak. You are pulled in to what could only be called "the conference call from Hell." The call was attended by at least 30 people of varying tactical, operational, technical, and managerial roles. I call it the "call from Hell" because it was simply this "mosh pit" of folks all trying to do the right thing but without any structure or discipline. Nobody on the call had any idea of what was going on other than computers throughout the company were sending enormous amounts of traffic trying to communicate with the Internet in a way that was not normal.

The organization detected the worm because the network utilization to the Internet was spiking with all this unusual traffic, and the number of machines broadcasting this traffic was increasing. The malicious code was spreading, and no one knew how or what it was doing to the actual machines it infected. Several formal organizational structures were in place in the company—InfoSec (information security), production support, and technical subject matter expert (SME) groups of all kinds, but none of those day-to-day organizations was organized or empowered to respond to a virus outbreak.

The call was polite but too chaotic for any real work to get done. Since Conficker was a new exploit, none of the infrastructure technology in place was helpful. Folks were asking, "What about AV (anti-virus) or IDS (intrusion detection systems)?" These signature-based technologies were useless for this kind of attack. With every new person joining the call, the collective would have to sit through the now relentless regurgitation of the crisis and the ensuing speculation as to cause and cure. So much was unknown at this time. And the calls to the AV vendor and other technology "experts" who were also entrusted with the security of this enterprise were to no avail, since they, too, were struggling to understand this new attack. As the virus started to move from the Asian group toward the North American hub, concern grew that it could start to affect core business operations.

Plenty of managers were involved, each with his or her particular area of responsibility, but no one was in charge. No one was officially tasked with managing this type of crisis. There was an increasing sense of alarm, and a sense of impotence started to manifest. I could almost sense lower level managers beginning to position themselves to prevent any finger-pointing in their direction. Then came the instant messages (IMs). Since the conference call, which now was droning on into its fourth hour, was producing no real solutions, folks (mostly technical) were starting to splinter off into IM groups to try to get something—anything—going.

The collective bumble sifted its way through various ideas. "What about containment? Let's cut off Asia to prevent this from spreading." But they realized that they had no idea how "cutting off Asia" would affect the rest of the business. They weren't even sure at the time how the virus was spreading. Would the cure be worse than the disease? Never mind that they didn't know much about the disease (other than it was still spreading). What about the various infected devices—laptops and PCs? Pull them off the network—that was easy. What about the file servers? Would it be worth taking a whole department off line? The virus was spreading, and everything was out of control. This was no longer about possibly making a bad decision. The collective lacked the ability to make *any* decision.

As information started to trickle in from the various vendors, friends, and industry contacts having the same issue in other companies, the technology infrastructure finally started to respond. The vulnerability was identified and the organization started its cumbersome process of rolling out patches. As more information about the threat became known and implemented in the various technologies within the company, AV and other technologies started delivering on their promises. Over time, the company was fortunate: although several hundred devices would be infected, the damage was minimal and repairable over time. The impact on the organization's network was mitigated largely by a technical SME who had enough of the conference call and took things into her own hands. As things settled, the clumsy collective was fortunate that it did not make matters worse and the impact to the business was minimal. They got lucky this time.

Think about the scenario for a moment before we move on to discuss some basic concepts of both crisis and planning.

Key Concepts

What follows are some basic concepts that are critical to understand before you can start the process of developing computer (or any crisis) incident response planning and execution. In later chapters, we'll discuss how your incident response plan will enable you to master many of the dynamics discussed here.

The OODA Loop

In the 1950s, the Air Force set out to understand the human cognitive process of its pilots. The result was called the "OODA loop," which is the foundation of contemporary information warfare.

OODA stands for four tasks: *observe*, *orient*, *decide*, and *act*. Whether we are preparing for battle or preparing to respond to a system breach, we are constantly *observing* our environment. We put these observations into some sort of context, often multiple contexts, to *orient* them as to how the observations might affect us. We then make *decisions* as to how to address, or if we even should address, these events. And, if necessary, we then take some *action*, even if that action is doing nothing.

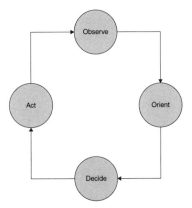

It's called an OODA *loop* because, typically, we want to see how our actions have impacted the events that were originally observed. Since this is an ongoing interaction, the OODA loop continues as long as we are cognitive.

Though this is a fairly simplistic description, this concept is important for you to understand, because during a time of crisis, an organization must be able to make a decision and take action. When writing plans to address risks, you need to address the sources of observation or input, and you must be able to put these events into context, make timely decisions, and ultimately provide the organization sufficient time and confidence to act; this is true for *every level of the organization*. If the organization is conducting top-down planning, then while the upper levels conduct their OODA process, they need to ensure that lower levels within the organization have sufficient time and resources to conduct their own subsequent OODA processes.

One example of how the OODA loop manifests in an organization is a concept that the military calls a "battle rhythm." A battle rhythm is grounded in the idea that within a "battle staff," certain prescribed events occur with predictability, so that all the various parties of the organization know what's expected of them and when. The battle rhythm also ensures that people are given time to do their jobs and report their results. The organization then needs time to review results and determine the next steps. The loop continues until the crisis is remediated.

Consider an operational/crisis cycle in which you expect members of your organization to meet, confer, and take action (via the OODA loop) every six hours. The group spends the first hour reviewing what it has observed, placing the observations into a context (such as business/technical impact), and then making decisions and assigning tasks. The remaining five hours is for subordinate groups to conduct their own OODA processes and ultimately to provide sufficient time for people to perform the actual work that "get things done." A battle rhythm in this context would involve status briefings at midnight, 6 A.M., noon, and 6 P.M. Assuming that each meeting takes an hour, five hours would remain for subordinate staffs to perform their own OODA loops and/or execute decisions. The six-hour rhythm is based on the balance of how frequently the management group needs to review progress versus allowing sufficient time for their decisions to be executed.

Fog of War

The second concept, the "fog of war," has been characterized by many military experts; simply put, in time of crisis, nobody knows what the heck is really going on and everyone is frantically trying to find out. This "fog" can be detrimental in several ways.

For example, suppose the leader during time of crisis wants to know all the information before he or she makes a decision. The result is that the leader will ultimately never make a decision because he or she will become stymied by the unknown. The second way this manifests is with well-intended individuals who begin to speculate and even panic, because there is no knowledge at present of what's going on in this crisis, what's causing it, or how it spreads. Lacking a good plan and a disciplined response, leaders risk watching as their organization spirals out of control; when ignorance pervades and speculation is undisciplined, they will seriously detract from the organization's ability to respond.

Friction

The third concept, friction, is the idea that during times of uncertainty, the variety of different views, opinions, ideas, and even agendas can cause paralysis, contention, and even downright hostility within an organization. Time, or more specifically, the lack of time, is also a major source of friction. (The fog of war, for example, can cause considerable friction.) Disputes occur as to who is responsible for what and who reports to whom, often because many corporations are not primarily organized to deal with crises. Friction is an inevitable factor in times of crisis; some would argue friction is a constant in any relationship, even without crisis. Whether you look at the Republicans versus Democrats, or IT versus business users, there will be day-to-day contention, even among individuals with the best of intentions. This becomes exaggerated in times of crisis.

Center of Gravity

The concept of "center of gravity" is most easily described by a few questions: What is the essence of your organization? What is it that your organization is or does that differentiates you to your customers and/or to your marketplace? What distinguishes you? What justifies your place in the market/society? The answers to these questions are important to know, because in time of crisis, quick decisions may need to be made and have the potential to impact the organization's ability to deliver those products or services that are your "center of gravity."

It's important that the members of the group responding to crisis on behalf of the organization truly understand what it is that they have to protect first and foremost. This may be your brand or your intellectual property. Implicit with risk is consequence.

How your CIRP manages consequences to your organization is heavily influenced by the understanding of this idea of center of gravity.

Unity of Command

One thing worse than bad decisions are no decisions. This bring us to "unity of command." With unity of command, all the varying dynamics of crisis and planning are held together by a single decision-making process. The organization is unified when it has the ability to make timely decisions, and when somebody is in command.

In many nonmilitary organizations, it may not be feasible for one person to be in command. And although I'm not a big proponent of decision by committee, because typically that's an oxymoron, some organizations prefer to make decisions this way, with representation from multiple areas of responsibility deciding collectively. You might form a "crisis committee" to make decisions during crises.

The key thing to remember is that whatever decision-making mechanism you put in place, it must be capable of making a decision during the fog of war and friction. You might need to create a committee with an odd number of people, to avoid a "hung jury" type stalemate. The key benefit of both unity of command as well as the OODA process is that the organization has the ability to make the difficult decisions in a timely manner.

Maintaining the Initiative

Security expert Jeff Klaben introduced this concept as "maintaining one's advantage." The military calls this "maintaining the initiative," and this is another concept that is imperative during planning and crisis execution. Maintaining the initiative in military perspective means you do your best to be out in front of the events. In the context of the battlefield, your enemy should be reacting to your actions, not vice versa. An organization can typically lose the initiative and become in a reactive, almost "free-for-all," mode when events aren't anticipated and the organization is unprepared for crisis. This is not to suggest that any amount of planning will ever create an environment in which the organization is calling all the shots in time of crisis. But the idea here is that with sufficient preparation, your organization can prepare for 80 percent of the anticipated needs, leaving itself with the resources and focus to address the 20 percent that will inevitably challenge the group.

Tactical, Operational, and Strategic Perspectives

Both the daily activities of your organization and during a time of crisis, three perspectives need to be addressed: tactical, operational, and strategic. The strategic perspective involves the board of directors, chief executive officer, and chief information officer. They will have opinions, concerns, and due diligence requirements that are of a strategic nature. Farther down in the organization, at the director and vice president level, operational concerns rule. Multiple units and divisions will need to work together to address the crisis. I believe one of the greatest struggles during time of crisis is the fact that most organizations at an operational level are not organized to deal with a specific crisis. And so one of the major objectives in your planning is to identify what tasks need to be accomplished and what ad hoc organization is necessary to accomplish those tasks. Finally at a tactical level, no matter how great your battle plans might be or how great the marketing strategy might be, at some point, somebody has to cross that line and make first contact either with your enemy or with your customer.

An important thing to understanding is that each of those different layers within the organization may have its own requirements for a form of OODA loop. And although you are spending precious minutes addressing strategic issues, you must provide sufficient time for the operational and tactical levels not only to have their own OODA loops, but most importantly, to have the time to complete the actions assigned to them.

Requirements-Driven Execution

"Requirements-driven execution" acknowledges that every organization has both statutory and contractual obligations, in addition to the basic due diligence obligations that executives have in protecting the business to maintain that "center of gravity." Requirements-driven execution starts with the identification of requirements that need to be satisfied in time of crisis. Whether it is a data breach, a phishing attack, a malware attack, or a food or product recall, the organization must satisfy certain obligations in time of crisis. In the middle of a crisis, the last thing you need is to be trying to figure out your obligations. These requirements will manifest at the strategic, operational, and tactical levels within the organization.

Matthew Todd wrote Chapter 2 of this book, which covers the numerous statutory, contractual, and industry best practices that are currently required of most U.S.-based organizations. As you start to digest this idea of requirements-based execution, or the greater concept of due diligence, Matthew's contribution will provide an exceptional foundation for the IT/InfoSec professional.

End State

"End state" is an articulated expectation of what success looks like. End state is typically a paragraph or two of the "five W's" (who, what, when, where, and why) and details what the organization defines as success. Some would argue that if you don't know what success is, you will have a difficult time achieving it. I would caution that getting a shared view of what success is can be very elusive. But at a minimum, you should have at least some sort of documented agreement as to what constitutes the termination of the crisis or termination of the response. Later in the book in Chapters 7 and 10, we will discuss incident termination guidelines.

Military Decision-Making Process

I have found the military decision-making process to be very advantageous over the years, and it also can assist with the enterprise risk management (ERM) focus that has been gaining considerable attention for Fortune 500 companies of late and also during a time of crisis.

The ability to make decisions is a basic requirement for any military officer, and most officers will go to a school to understand how it's done in the military. I don't intend to get too far into the details here, but the concept is pretty basic, assuming you have a problem to solve or an objective to accomplish.

Various groups or resources may be available to help you solve this problem (or more specifically to achieve the end state). You task your team with developing three distinct recommendations that will achieve the objective. When the three courses of action are presented, the group collectively critiques each course of action from each source's respective area of expertise. In doing this, you identify the various advantages and risks of each option. Then, the leader, the decision-making body, or the collective decide which is the best option to execute.

This process facilitates a more risk-aware organization, forces more creativity, and creates a greater sense of inclusion in the planning process. Also, with input from the various experts in the group, you can identify major risk factors that need to be considered and addressed. I believe this decision-making methodology is an important point of discussion, because, again, during a time of crisis, you need to have as much consistency and discipline as possible

NOTE

If you are interested in this topic, I recommend that you review the military publication titled "FM 5-0 Army Planning and Orders Production." As more organizations come to embrace ERM and develop a more risk-aware consciousness within their organization, the military decision-making methodology will serve them well.

Foreword

A Plan Is Preparation Manifested

Sound Information Security Management principles suggest that all organizations entrusted to maintain the Confidentiality, Integrity, and Availability of sensitive data should incorporate Protective, Detective, and Corrective measures to ensure such a result. Planning is a corrective mechanism and should be part of any Information Security effort. For planning to be an effective corrective mechanism it must provide a solid foundation as to its execution, specific information so that participants are empowered with current and relevant knowledge, and yet be broad as to not constrict an organization's ability to respond to unforeseen events. Planning will rarely answer all the questions that come up during an incident, but it should provide a repository of thoughtful *anticipation*, *collaboration*, and *research*. Furthermore, to assure a plan's continued usefulness, it should be tested and updated on a regular basis. A plan's true value is measured by the relevance of the information and processes it provides at a time of crisis.

A Plan Is Preparation Manifested

At this point, I will introduce you to the first of what will be many references to the working CIRPs that I am including as part of this book. As I mentioned at the beginning of this chapter, all of my CIRPs start with a foreword with two major sections. I'll begin by discussing the first section.

This is the first full paragraph that anyone who reads my plans will see. I believe it is important that the reader understand the premise of the document they are about to read. In reading this, I hope that they will come to appreciate the effort that went into producing this CIRP document and the effort that is required to maintain the document. I also hope that it will establish some expectations about the plan itself.

They should appreciate that the plan is executable. I can't tell you how many plans and planning books I have read that lack the ability to be immediately executable. The plan should be a thoroughly documented repository for three major components: anticipation, collaboration, and research.

Anticipation: Objectives and Requirements

Anticipation is strongly linked to requirements-driven execution. You must anticipate the requirements that will need to be met in the event of the computer incident you are addressing. You'll need to identify the decisions that must be made and any necessary resources needed to support those requirements. You should detail all of the objectives and requirements as part of your first steps in producing any plan for responding to a crisis.

Collaboration: Socialization and Normalization

Socialization and normalization are the major components of collaboration. *Socialization* is based on the idea that we must share these plans not just within our immediate organization—whether it be InfoSec or IT—but throughout the organization and even to third parties. Socialization is important because it gives others the opportunity to provide input and criticism but also implicit sponsorship of your plan. Much like a business plan, a CIRP is an excellent vehicle for soliciting and capturing numerous perspectives within the organization. *Normalization* is the process by which others in the organization help you make your plan work within the various nuances and norms of the organization. It's amazing how, when you reach out to others within your organization, you come to learn "how things are really done here." We'll revisit this topic in greater detail in Chapter 4's discussion of the CIRP Advisory Committee.

Research: The Availability of Relevant Information

I'm a big believer that relevant information must be immediately available. This information will be needed by the CIRP group responding to crisis. You may also need it for third parties such as law enforcement, a PCI forensic investigator (PFI—previously known as Qualified Incident Response Assessors, or QIRAs), and/or lawyers. The value of timely and relevant information cannot be understated. This goes back to this concept of maintaining the initiative. It is very difficult to maintain the initiative at time of crisis when you are chasing down information that you could have easily had anticipated and prepared as part of your plan.

The Ad Hoc Organization for Time of Crisis

In order for a plan to be relevant, it needs to be immediately executable. The various participants of your plan need to understand their roles, the resources they will have available, and the battle rhythm of this new crisis. Depending on the structure of your organization, you may not be properly organized to respond to a specific crisis. One of the key deliverables in any immediately executable CIRP is the development of an ad hoc organization to respond to the incident immediately. Your current organization may not be structured to respond adequately to this low probability, high impact event. This is one of the things that socialization, normalization, and identifying requirements will help you with as you identify resources and obligations, and structure them in an ad hoc fashion to respond to your crisis. We will discuss this topic in much greater detail in Chapters 6 and 9 of this book.

The Value of Documentation

One final point about documentation. There's a saying that "if it's not documented, it's not real." Chapter 3 goes into much greater detail about getting even more benefits from a well-documented plan, but, frankly speaking, if you're an IT or InfoSec professional and you think that you can simply wing it in time of crisis, you are doing yourself and the people who depend on you a disservice.

Yes, it takes a lot of effort to create and maintain CIRPs. We all know that when you document and share this kind of information, you expose yourself to criticism, and some folks don't like being professionally vulnerable. But the age-old excuse of "it's all in my head and I just don't have the time to write down" will deprive your organization of the many benefits that come from a documented plan. Documentation is the very foundation upon which all of these other benefits can be applied. But you must start with a documented plan; even a poor plan that is documented is better than a great plan in someone's head.

One of the most valuable benefits or byproducts of a well-documented response plan is the assurance that you can give others in the organization that you have performed your due diligence to mitigate and/or respond to these specific risks.

Cyber Due Diligence in an Era of Information Risk

Any modern enterprise—from the smallest mom-and-pop store to the largest corporation—understands the need for basic information security, especially when it comes to computer systems. One bad virus outbreak can tie up IT organizations (or your nephew Bobby who is *so* good with computers) for days—not to mention the possibility of lost clients or bad publicity in the case of a serious malware attack. Thankfully, a host of solutions exists for every enterprise, large or small, including anti-virus and anti-malware software, data loss prevention (DLP) systems, network intrusion detection/network intrusion prevention systems (NIDS/NIPS), host intrusion detection/host intrusion protection systems (HIDS/HIPS), on-premises systems, cloud-based systems, and guaranteed magical systems protection services. There's a tool for every problem and a vendor for every tool.

Various standards can help businesses establish a framework for identifying and managing risk, but since such good tools are available, why bother with this? Regrettably, every tool might do well with whatever it is specifically designed to tackle, but a tool often falls flat on its face when confronted with the real world of simultaneous viruses, system design failures, and systems administrators with the flu. Tools can be improperly installed, inadequately managed or maintained, or even missing from entire segments of a corporate network. Staff can be inadequately prepared or trained to respond when the alarms go off. Breaches can still occur through avenues not even contemplated by the best tools—such as a properly authorized employee accessing confidential information in the course of his regular business activities, despite the fact that he was fired two days earlier. A sound framework for risk management could help you identify and close such gaps.

Fear of failure or of the unknown risk can be good motivators for adopting standards, but there are others. Ultimately, most (if not all) businesses will be compelled by external forces to adopt standards. Some of these external forces are outlined in the sections that follow.

Regulation

In response to inconsistent adoption of sound information security and privacy practices, various state and federal regulatory agencies have mandated that standards of information security and risk management be adopted by the industries those agencies oversee. Ultimately, regulation attempts to make it clear to regulated businesses that sensitive data must be properly protected, and it identifies what constitutes minimum standards of data protection. Following are some examples.

Gramm-Leach-Bliley Act
(Financial Services Modernization Act of 1999)

The Gramm-Leach-Bliley Act (GLBA) regulates banks, brokerages, insurance companies, and other U.S. financial institutions, and compliance is mandatory. Section 501 of GLBA (15 U.S.C. §§ 6801) obliges financial institutions not only "to protect the security and confidentiality of…customers' nonpublic personal information," but also for regulators specifically to…

> …establish appropriate standards for the financial institutions subject to their jurisdiction relating to administrative, technical, and physical safeguards—
>
> ► to ensure the security and confidentiality of customer records and information;
>
> ► to protect against any anticipated threats or hazards to the security or integrity of such records; and
>
> ► to protect against unauthorized access to or use of such records or information which could result in substantial harm or inconvenience to any customer.

Various federal agencies have published guidelines that intend to establish or clarify the standards for information security. For example, the Office of the Comptroller of the Currency, Board of Governors of the Federal Reserve System, Federal Deposit Insurance Corporation, and Office of Thrift Supervision collectively published *Interagency Guidelines Establishing Standards for Safeguarding Customer Information and Rescission of Year 2000 Standards for Safety and Soundness* (www.federalregister .gov/articles/2001/02/01/01-1114/interagency-guidelines-establishing-standards-for-safeguarding-customer-information-and-rescission) in 2001, and, later, the *Small-Entity Compliance Guide* (www.federalreserve.gov/bankinforeg/interagencyguidelines.htm) that offers an easy-to-read overview of the guidelines. Similarly, the Securities and Exchange Commission adopted Regulation S-P (Privacy of Consumer Financial Information), including "Safeguard Procedures" based on section 501.

The Health Insurance Portability and Accountability Act of 1996

The Health Insurance Portability and Accountability Act of 1996 (HIPAA) requires that health care providers, health plans, and health care clearinghouses (and, with the introduction of the Health Information Technology for Economic and Clinical

Health [HITECH] Act, their business associates) ensure the security and privacy of private health information.

The U.S. Department of Health and Human Services issued a Final Rule on Security Standards (www.hhs.gov/ocr/privacy/hipaa/administrative/securityrule/securityrulepdf.pdf) in 2003, which provides several general requirements. Covered entities must do the following:

▶ Ensure the confidentiality, integrity, and availability of all electronic protected health information the covered entity creates, receives, maintains, or transmits.

▶ Protect against any reasonably anticipated threats or hazards to the security or integrity of such information.

▶ Protect against any reasonably anticipated uses or disclosures of such information that are not permitted or required under subpart E of this part.

▶ Ensure compliance with this subpart by its workforce.

The Final Rule on Security Standards then describes specific administrative, physical, and technical safeguards that covered entities must employ.

⚔ Sarbanes-Oxley Act of 2002

The Sarbanes-Oxley Act established or updated standards for public companies in the wake of the financial scandals of Enron, Tyco, and others between 2000 and 2002. Section 404 of the Act requires that public companies or their auditors assess and report on the effectiveness of the company's internal controls; although these controls are meant to cover financial statements, they naturally extend more broadly, including general risk assessment and governance, IT controls and management, and hiring and termination. The Public Company Accounting Oversight Board is the primary regulator overseeing audits of public companies, and it adopted Auditing Standard No. 5 (http://pcaobus.org/Standards/Auditing/Pages/Auditing_Standard_5.aspx) in 2007, which describes standards for auditors, including a top-down risk assessment, how to assess risk and materiality, and examples of risks and controls.

State Breach Requirements

State regulators have adopted various regulations concerning breaches of confidential personal data, and, in doing so, have mandated standards for those entities that handle or process such data. These regulations generally cover entities doing business within those states or handling private data of those states' residents. For example,

Massachusetts 201 CMR 17.00 (www.mass.gov/Eoca/docs/idtheft/201CMR1700reg
.pdf) "establishes minimum standards to be met in connection with the safeguarding
of personal information contained in both paper and electronic records" for
those "persons who own or license personal information about a resident of the
Commonwealth of Massachusetts." The standards include both a "comprehensive
information security program" and specific "computer systems security requirements."
(Massachusetts has provided a "Compliance Checklist" at www.mass.gov/Eoca/docs/
idtheft/compliance_checklist.pdf to help entities comply with the regulation.)

Industry Standards

In a small number of cases, industries have established their own standards for
information security. The best known is the Payment Card Industry Data Security
Standard (PCI DSS) (www.pcisecuritystandards.org/security_standards/index.php),
established and maintained by the PCI Security Standards Council. PCI DSS
"provides an actionable framework for developing a robust payment card data security
process—including prevention, detection, and appropriate reaction to security incidents."

The Air Transport Association has published the "Aviation Industry Standards for
Digital Information Security" (https://publications.airlines.org/CommerceProductDetail
.aspx?Product=108), which provides standards for secure communications.

Federal/State Enforcement

When a regulator enforces a regulation against a company, the enforcement action
may include a requirement that the company adopt various standards and provide
evidence of such adoption. Although this does not mean that the regulation requires
these standards, it serves as a warning to other entities: either adopt these standards,
or they may be imposed should the regulator become involved.

Consider, for example, the actions of the Federal Trade Commission (FTC) against
data-aggregation company ChoicePoint (www.ftc.gov/opa/2006/01/choicepoint.shtm).
In 2005, ChoicePoint acknowledged a breach of private records for more than
163,000 individuals. In investigating the case, the FTC charged that the breach
demonstrated that the company "violated the FTC Act by making false and misleading
statements about its privacy policies." The FTC order required that ChoicePoint
"establish, implement, and maintain a comprehensive information security program
designed to protect the security, confidentiality, and integrity of the personal
information it collects from or about consumers," and undergo an independent audit of
its security program every two years to provide evidence of compliance with the order.

In April 2008, ChoicePoint suffered another data breach after it disabled a key database monitor, which it reported to the FTC (www.ftc.gov/opa/2009/10/choicepoint .shtm). The FTC amended its earlier court order to compel the organization "to report to the FTC—every two months for two years—detailed information about how it is protecting the breached database and certain other databases and records containing personal information."

Contractual Enforcement

In some cases, regulations require regulated entities to ensure that their vendors adopt comparable standards where sensitive data is involved. For example, in the Interagency Guidelines Establishing Information Security Standards (www.federalreserve.gov/ bankinforeg/interagencyguidelines.htm), financial institutions must "require, by contract, service providers that have access to its customer information to take appropriate steps to protect the security and confidentiality of this information." Massachusetts 201 CMR 17.00 (www.mass.gov/Eoca/docs/idtheft/ 201CMR1700reg.pdf) requires entities to oversee third-party service providers and establish contractual requirements with them "to implement and maintain...appropriate security measures for personal information."

Even in the absence of regulatory requirements, many businesses build requirements into contracts to ensure that their vendors take adequate precautions. Such precautions are obviously appropriate when a vendor has access to sensitive financial, health, or other personal information of individuals, but even the most innocuous vendors may have access to sensitive information in the form of banking information (for wire transfers), lists of key personnel (for business contacts), or even knowledge of business plans. It may not be enough to have a nondisclosure agreement in place if the vendor has no means to educate its personnel and enforce its obligations, and a contract can be used to enforce appropriate standards covering those areas.

What Standards?

Regulations and contracts generally require entities to adopt appropriate standards to protect confidential information, but they rarely provide specific requirements. Thankfully, a number of standards and other tools exist to provide comprehensive frameworks for a security practice, and although they are not prescriptive, they help entities ask the right questions, cover the right areas, and establish the right processes for their particular circumstances.

⍟ –/+ ISO/IEC 27000 Series

The International Organization for Standardization (ISO) and the International Electrotechnical Commission (IEC) published a series of standards for information security management systems called the "ISO/IEC 27000 series," available from the ANSI eStandards Store (http://webstore.ansi.org/). It provides an overview of the series (in ISO/IEC 27000 itself) and a number of other standards (27001, 27002, and so on) covering such areas as the following:

- ▶ **27001**   Information security management systems—Requirements
- ▶ **27002**   Code of practice for information security management
- ▶ **27003**   Information security management system implementation guidance
- ▶ **27004**   Information security management—Measurement
- ▶ **27005**   Information security risk management
- ▶ **27006**   Requirements for bodies providing audit and certification of information security management systems

ISO/IEC 27002 provides a comprehensive list of 12 sections, each with a set of security controls and objectives, and ISO/IEC 27001 provides a framework in which those controls would operate in a cohesive manner. Although there is some general discussion of risk identification and management in ISO/IEC 27002, ISO/IEC 27005 provides greater detail. An entity could use a combination of these three standards to help establish a comprehensive and dynamic process to identify risks and appropriate controls across the enterprise.

FFIEC

The Federal Financial Institutions Examination Council (FFIEC) is an interagency body that prescribes uniform principles, standards, and report forms for the federal examination of financial institutions. It has published a series of IT examination booklets (http://ithandbook.ffiec.gov/it-booklets.aspx) that provide standards and education for field examiners in a wide variety of topics, including information security (http://ithandbook.ffiec.gov/it-booklets/information-security.aspx). The standards in the information security booklet serve as a supplement to GLBA and provide a reasonably comprehensive overview of governance and control objectives (especially for financial institutions, but applicable to other entities as well).

PCI DSS

As mentioned, PCI DSS provides standards for entities that process credit card data. Although the PCI standards are meant to aid in the protection of cardholder data, they apply to other sensitive data as well—control objective areas include policy, network security, access control, monitoring, and testing. The PCI DSS web site (www.pcisecuritystandards.org/) includes a number of guideline documents with specific guidance for many of the control objectives that are designed to help entities achieve compliance with the standard.

PCI DSS does not cover such areas as governance, human resources, risk assessment, and other less–IT-centric control objectives.

Service Organization Controls

Service Organization Controls (SOC) reports (www.aicpa.org/interestareas/frc/assuranceadvisoryservices/pages/serviceorganization%27smanagement.aspxt) replace the SAS-70 (SOC 1) and SysTrust (SOC 2 and SOC 3) attestation standards and are provided by a certified public accountant after an audit. The SOC 2 and SOC 3 "are intended to meet the needs of a broad range of users that need information and assurance about the controls at a service organization" and can cover one or more of five principles (security, availability, processing integrity, confidentiality and/or privacy). Each of the principles has a prescribed set of control objectives that entities can use as a set of standards for risk management in that principle area, as well as more general standards including policy, training, and ongoing maintenance.

Shared Assessments

The Shared Assessments Program (www.sharedassessments.org/about) was originally developed by financial institutions, accounting firms, and service providers to provide a consistent framework for evaluating service providers. The program provides the Standardized Information Gathering Questionnaire (SIG) and the Agreed Upon Procedures (AUP), both of which were developed and are maintained based upon existing standards such as the ISO/IEC 27000 series, PCI DSS, and FFIEC guidelines (ww.sharedassessments.org/about/programtools.html). The SIG gives entities a consistent tool to assess risks at their own service providers, and the AUP provides a tool for an entity to assess their own risk. An entity may also share the AUP report with its clients and potentially reduce or eliminate the need for clients to perform their own assessments of the entity.

How Do I Know that I'm Doing the Right Thing?

Even the most sophisticated enterprises with the most careful conformance to standards can be breached. Standards may not be applied everywhere or may not be applied consistently. Service providers may have gaps that present a material risk. Without some means of assessment, it is difficult to know if standards are being adhered to, applied consistently, or actually mitigating risk.

It is essential to remember that internal or external teams or vendors will assess only those areas they are told to assess, and that, in most cases, they must trust that the entity does what it claims to do. If areas for assessment are limited by the defined scope or available resources, or if teams or service providers being tested attempt to cover up areas of weakness or provide "point in time" controls that are not consistently applied, risks may remain, and the entity must be prepared to deal with those risks. (This book is a good place to start!)

Independent Review

Independent auditors with proper expertise or accreditation can assess entities for compliance to external standards (for example, ISO/IEC 27000-series, SOC 1, 2, or 3, or PCI DSS), and (if properly accredited) provide independent reports for clients, investors, or other associated parties that rely on the entity. Independent auditors must rely on the entity to provide adequate access and system or control description to provide a review, while the entity must be sure the control areas adequately cover areas of risk about which the entity or other interested parties may be concerned.

Internal Audit

External auditors are typically engaged once or twice a year due to the cost and scope of an engagement. A strong internal audit team can provide more frequent or comprehensive benefit to an entity than an external auditor (but obviously cannot provide the independence required for an external report). If properly established with appropriate independence, authorization, and resources, an internal audit team can use external or internal standards as well as a more intimate knowledge of the business to assess risks and provide guidance more frequently and more deeply than is typical of an external engagement.

Internal audit need not be a formal team with a charter—it could instead be a periodic process of self-assessment, either against internal standards or policies, or even using a tool such as the AUP. Formal or not, the process of internal control review requires an owner, with a specific charter to ensure that controls are reviewed at an appropriate interval.

Tabletop Exercises

It is important to remember that audits test controls that are typically designed to mitigate known *individual* risks—in other words, controls are commonly tested to be sure they mitigate one risk at a time. For example, a company might have defined a control around the failure of an e-mail server, where backup systems automatically take over and procedures are defined for recovery. The company might do an excellent job of testing this control by inducing a failure on an e-mail server, confirm that the control works as defined, and be satisfied with the result. Unfortunately, system failures rarely happen in isolation—what if the e-mail server failure was actually caused by a virus that also corrupted the database that the backup systems rely upon? What if the key e-mail administrator is out of commission at the same time?

Periodic "mock disasters" provide internal teams with another way to test controls and recovery processes that might go well beyond the scope of standards or audits. They can vary in size and scope, from regularly scheduled 20-minute team exercises led by a manager to much more sophisticated cross-functional exercises that span several hours, led by a coordinator, with formal "injects" and an after-review.

Exercises can satisfy many objectives for an enterprise. They engage team members that might not otherwise be fighting fires on a regular basis and keep them sharp. They serve as safe tests of disaster plans. They reinforce communications protocols and test their effectiveness. They can even provide evidence to executives or board members of team preparedness for risks that are of particular interest.

How Do I Keep It Up?

Internal standards and controls grow stale with time as the business or environment changes around them. Entities need to establish a framework for periodic review and maintenance, and ensure ownership and oversight of the process—ownership to ensure that the review occurs on a regular basis, and oversight to be sure the standards and controls are reviewed in light of current business strategy, changing client expectations, competitive pressures, new technology, the operating business environment, regulatory updates, and any other relevant factors. Several recognized frameworks exist.

COBIT

COBIT (www.isaca.org/Knowledge-Center/COBIT/Pages/Overview.aspx) is a framework for IT governance and controls, established and maintained by ISACA (www.isaca.org). It is focused on proper alignment of IT processes with business objectives, assessment of the performance and maturity of the IT processes, and identification of responsibilities of associated business process owners. For IT processes, it serves as an aggregate of other practices or standards such as the Information Technology Infrastructure Library (ITIL), the ISO/IEC 27000 series, and Capability Maturity Model Integration (CMMI).

ISO/IEC 27005 (Information Security Risk Management)

Although not prescriptive about the method, ISO/IEC 27005 provides a framework for the analysis and management of risk and can be used as part of a framework for identifying and mitigating risk and assessing and updating controls. It is part of the ISO/IEC 27000 series of information security standards.

ITIL

ITIL (www.itil-officialsite.com/home/home.asp) was developed by the United Kingdom as a set of best practices meant to be tailored to an individual company's requirements. According to the ITIL official web site, "It provides a practical, no-nonsense framework for identifying, planning, delivering, and supporting IT services to the business."

Bringing It Together

Agility is a hallmark of current business—either get going or get out of the way. Standards seem antithetical to agility; they are perceived as roadblocks rather than aids for the modern business. It takes some vision, and perhaps some real-world examples of failures (ideally, not at your own firm), to demonstrate the purpose and effectiveness of standards for your business.

There are only a few opportunities for an operations manager, risk manager, or even the Board of Directors to introduce the idea of standards into an enterprise. Obviously, the start of a new enterprise is the best time to incorporate the concept of standards, but other key events can serve as leverage points as well—the start of a new line of business, the roll out of the first major client, or even after the first major failure. If you have the opportunity to introduce the idea, here are a few areas for consideration.

Top-Down Approval

Without top-down approval, establishing and maintaining a standards-based program is doomed to failure. If senior management does not appreciate the value of standards, few resources will be dedicated to them, and it will be significantly more difficult for you to stay on top of requirements from both the business and external factors.

To "sell" the adoption of standards within the business to the C-suite, you would be wise to gain a key ally, such as the CFO or chief counsel. Both of these C-level executives likely have experience with standards that impact their areas of responsibility, such as Sarbanes-Oxley or relevant industry regulations. In some cases, you may find one or more allies on the board of directors, especially if an audit committee exists. In any case, work with your allies to promote the idea that adopting appropriate standards, policies, and procedures within the enterprise will ultimately make the business more robust and resistant to failure. Be prepared with clear examples of how standards can be used to establish applicable policies and controls for the enterprise, measurements that the C-suite can use to monitor the effectiveness of the controls, and protection from failure.

Values

It is critical for the C-suite to establish compliance with standards and policies as a key corporate value. This can be stated in a variety of ways—for example, by incorporating compliance into the corporate value statement, by establishing a compliance department with a specific charter and budget to educate and enforce across the enterprise, or by establishing a "culture of excellence" with clear goals to establish and maintain standards appropriate to the business. If the C-suite properly establishes such values, business units will incorporate standards into their practices, quarterly goals will reflect the standards, and individuals will be aware of those standards that pertain to them and against which they are measured and compensated.

Sometimes, values are necessarily high-level and not specific, but it is critical to understand how they are meant to be interpreted. For example, a bank might state that it desires to be "trusted," and the C-suite understands that compliance with various federal and state financial standards are critical in demonstrating that trust.

Policies

Policies are the first place in a business where standards are made real for the business. Without clear policies, business units and individuals have no basis to know what is or is not allowed within the organization. Policies establish a framework for the business on which an overall practice is maintained, including education, enforcement, monitoring, measurement, and maintenance. Policies are ultimately the internal standards for the business.

Various policies are written or updated based on business requirements and applicable external standards. Here, the ISO/IEC 27002 standards, the SOC control objectives, and the AUP can provide frameworks for policy documents and ensure coverage of many areas (particularly for information security and technology standards), but applicable federal or state regulations should be consulted as well. Keep in mind that external standards can impact many of your internal policies, including information security, human resources, and ethics policies.

Ownership

Clear ownership of policies, procedures, and actual practice must be established and generally occurs at the business process level (establishing "business process owners"). Without clear owners of various control objectives, those objectives will not be met. Owners should be given appropriate authority and oversight over their control areas and should be compensated based on how they help to meet corporate objectives of compliance with internal and external standards. Policymakers should carefully consider the input from business process owners when policies are written and updated to ensure that policies are appropriate and actionable.

Ultimately, ownership should be properly reflected in the management structure, with policymakers, business process owners, and risk managers having appropriate levels of authority within the organization as a whole. Appropriate reporting structures will ensure that they are given the resources, direction, and compensation they require to perform their functions effectively.

Procedures and Controls

Business teams should establish procedures, controls, and measurements based on business process objectives and internal policies. Written procedures make up a "run book" that can be used to train new personnel and can even be used to ensure efficiency by periodic review. Controls should be placed to minimize failure without unduly slowing the process at hand, be automated where possible, and incorporate business process owner approvals where appropriate.

Measurement and Monitoring

Measurements of performance and efficiency can be placed within business processes and at key points throughout the enterprise to help business units meet key goals and to help management and auditors ensure compliance. Appropriate monitors of control points (such as key stakeholder approval within a business process) are critical for external audit teams during ISO/IEC, SOC, or PCI audits, and can make the process of undergoing an external audit go significantly more smoothly. Performance metrics and compliance monitors can also be used by the business to ensure that service levels are met, to identify key blockages in business processes, or to improve internal standards, process documents, or training regimens.

Education

Education is a key part of any standards program. Individual employees or contractors need not know every standard that applies to the business, but they do need to understand the purpose of those policies and standards that apply to their line of work (to be able to make sound business decisions, for example), and receive specific training on those procedures and controls that impact their jobs. A well-informed individual worker should know not only exactly what to do, but why it is important to do so in a particular manner. Engaging workers in this way helps them to understand the motivation behind the controls and can even allow them to see better ways to achieve the control objectives and ultimately improve the business. It also allows them to react to unexpected occurrences with an appropriate perspective—if an individual worker understands the corporate standard around the protection of client data, and an e-mail is unintentionally forwarded to her/his mailbox, the worker will know how to respond. + familiarity

Calendar for Testing Processes and Controls

Periodic internal testing helps to ensure that processes and controls do not get stale. Such testing can be performed by a dedicated internal audit team, a cross-functional internal team (such as a risk management committee), an external consultant, or even individual business process owners (at the direction of their management). Testing should ensure that applicable external standards are being followed (consulting with internal or external expert teams, such as the compliance department), that control objectives are being met, that new business standards or technology are appropriately considered, and that performance standards are being met. Appropriate intervals for testing should be established based on the apparent risks, the frequency of change of the environment (standards, business, or technology), and the impact on the business process or control being tested.

Independent Review

From time to time, a top-to-bottom review should be performed. Policies are necessarily designed to be robust and require infrequent updates, but they should always properly reflect the current applicable external standards and the business's operating environment, and they should be reviewed at least annually. The organizational structure should be reviewed to ensure that appropriate resources and authority are assigned to ensure that objectives are being met. These types of reviews can be performed by an appropriately independent internal audit team or by an external auditor or consultant. The results of such review should be provided in a formal report to the C-suite or audit committee of the board of directors.

Internal Oversight

To round out a successful program of standards compliance, it should be rolled into a formal risk management practice overseen by a risk management committee. This committee should comprise representatives from all business units, whose representatives have the authority and responsibility to promote appropriate activities within their respective business units while representing their various business requirements and responsibilities to the committee. The committee should also have representative experts for matters of policy and standards compliance. Ultimately, the risk committee can oversee the activities of the standards program, identify key risks and appropriate mitigating controls, report to the C-suite and Board, and ensure the successful operation of the overall program.

PART
II

Planning for Crisis

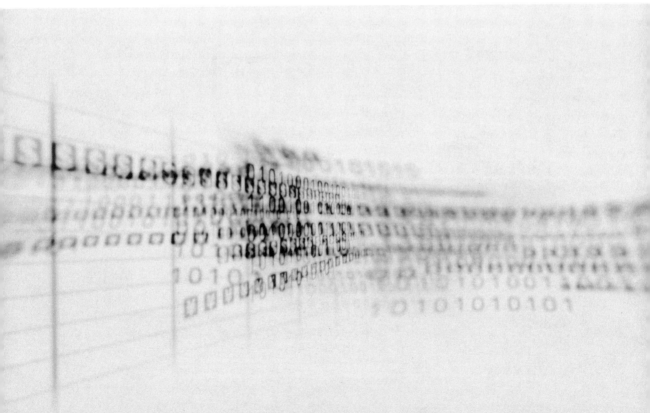

CHAPTER 3

Getting More
Out of Your Plans

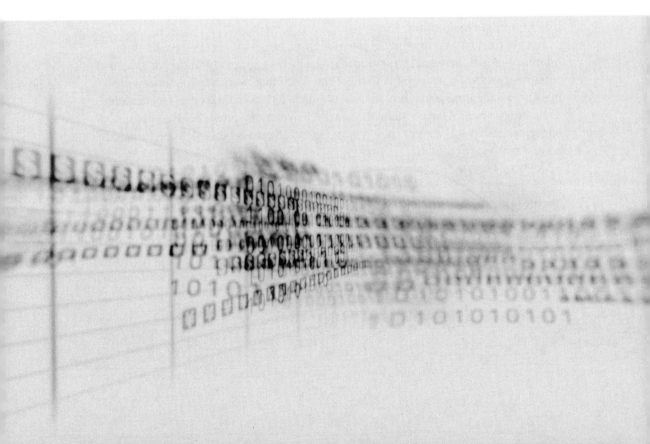

I n this chapter, I'll discuss the additional value of incident response plans in addition to mitigating certain risks. As discussed in Matthew Todd's Chapter 2, the standard of due diligence for information security management is a moving target at best. Information security professionals must regularly perform tasks that establish due diligence in the protection of their organization. A documented plan creates an opportunity to demonstrate to management, auditors, and individuals that the organization is maintaining a standard of due care.

The effort you put into your plan to socialize and normalize all the issues considered in previous chapters should become evident to any knowledgeable person who is reviewing the plan. This will show that you have taken your due-dilegence obligations seriously.

Proactively Using Plans During Period of Heightened Risk

A well-articulated Computer Incident Response Plan (CIRP) can be used proactively to prevent a crisis from escalating unnecessarily. The following is a real-world example of how a documented malware response plan was used proactively to create considerable benefit for the organization.

It was clear that our organization was a prime target and at severe risk of an imminent global malware infestation. We detailed several criteria that made our enterprise extremely vulnerable to the virus. With that rationale, I activated the malware incident response protocol. In boldface letters in the computer incident declaration e-mail, I wrote that we were not currently infected, but that I believed our organization was at very high risk of being infected by this virus and I listed several reasons for this.

An hour later, we had a conference call with the entire malware incident response team. Instead of reacting to a malware infection, we used the opportunity and our resources to ensure that all the applicable technologies we had installed in our enterprise were properly updated and ready to confront this virus. All the appropriate resources were on the call and ready to respond should we see any indication that the virus had entered our network. We quickly put out a dispatch to senior management to be aware of this potential virus, and to let them know that we had already coordinated resources to respond to it.

As a result, for the first time ever, we were able to mobilize and deal with a malware outbreak proactively. We would later read in the media that this virus was the biggest e-mail worm attack in almost ten years. It was actually a worm developed and deployed by a quasi-terrorist organization called Iraq Resistance and was sent in response to the U.S. invasion of Iraq and the activities of a radical Florida pastor named Terry Jones. This virus affected many large organizations, such as AIG, Comcast, Disney, NASA, and Proctor and Gamble.

This is just one example of how the proactive use of an incident response plan helped to prevent a risk from significantly impacting an organization. Although it may be contrary to some of the conventional wisdom out there, a CIRP can be useful for more than just reacting to problems.

Understanding How Your ISOC Works

A CIRP can provide a better understanding of how your Information Security Operations Center (ISOC) works—or, if you don't have an ISOC, a CIRP can show you how all the various operational flows of all that InfoSec data *should* work. Because the plan you are developing will deal with specific threats or risks, you need to develop a very detailed understanding of the various precursors, alerts, and other mechanisms that may notify you that you have a crisis and also document these in your plan (as discussed in greater detail in Chapters 5 and 8). The exercise of documenting this information will help you gain a complete understanding of whether your current ISOC operational processes are sufficient to address the risks.

Here's another real-world example that shows how you might find an additional benefit of understanding how key information can flow in and out of your information security organization.

During our annual PCI audit, the auditor who was reviewing our "Data Breach" CIRP asked, "Don't you guys have an 800-ethics hotline that employees can call in on?" I hated to admit this, but I didn't know the answer. The logic of the auditor was that if an employee had knowledge that another employee was hacking the system or stealing credit card numbers, the suspicious employee could call the ethics line to report it.

This was more than just "something missing in the CIRP." This had implications for the way our ISOC interfaced with the rest of the organization and how effective our InfoSec organization could be at responding to such a threat. Based on that auditor's question, I chased down the 800-ethics line, spoke to the person in corporate security (loss prevention) who answered the call, and established a mechanism to link and forward any relevant ethics hotline notifications to the ISOC. I also updated the CIRP to include the ethics hotline as a possible source of detection/notification of a breach or other malicious activity.

Building Relationships Outside of IT

Your efforts in developing CIRPs offer you a tremendous vehicle for developing valuable relationships outside of IT. This has been by far the greatest benefit for me personally.

As you will see in later chapters, most incident responses involve people outside of InfoSec, and in many cases, outside of IT. But these need not be one-time encounters. Whether you are maintaining the currency of your plan(s), testing your plan(s) annually, or regularly executing the plan(s), your ongoing contact with various individuals is critical to maintaining a plan that is immediately executable.

In my organization, I average one CIRP execution on an almost quarterly basis. Because many of the participants work outside of InfoSec and IT, I have developed great working relationships with these folks. Over the years of supporting these plans, I have worked with people in the corporate legal, finance, public affairs, corporate security (loss prevention), and corporate insurance. Collaborating with and knowing these individuals can be a tremendous benefit to an information security professional; they can help you see the larger organizational picture and understand the variety of endeavors that take place outside of your "InfoSec/IT bubble."

Leveraging Your CIRP to Develop Relationships with Law Enforcement

Many CIRPs that address the potential of criminal misconduct require anticipation, collaboration, and research involving law enforcement. Building and maintaining a CIRP is an excellent opportunity to reach out to local law enforcement resources. (Starting with Chapter 5, I'll discuss this in greater detail.)

If you are an InfoSec or IT person, you should probably work with your corporate security (physical security/fraud) group, because they may already have a working relationship with law enforcement. This is a key opportunity: At a time of crisis, you don't want be the one trying to figure out who to call and how. You might think it's as easy as dialing 9-1-1, but that's not realistic. Truth is, the 9-1-1 operator might not be prepared to deal with cyber-crime. Many states have regional law enforcement teams specifically designed to handle cyber-crime, and this is something you should know about. Consider, for example, the Northern California Computer Crimes Task Force (NC3TF). This is a special group of local law enforcement personnel who receive cyber-specific training and work only with cyber-crimes. They are usually made up of police officers from local police departments and investigators from the district attorney's office in the counties that are covered by this task force.

If you are an InfoSec professional working in a community with a computer crimes task force, you should make an effort to reach out to them. Many of these groups are eager to understand their constituency and eager to help you. The NC3TF, for example, hosts quarterly meetings that are open to the members of the public with security roles.

In addition, national level resources of the FBI and the U.S. Secret Service (USSS) have jurisdiction over cyber-crime. In most major U.S. cities, the USSS hosts quarterly Electronic Crimes Task Force (ECTF) meetings with the public, and the FBI has a public outreach program called InfraGard. InfraGard usually comprises local individuals from the private sector and the non–law enforcement public sector and typically meets quarterly. Both of these forums are great opportunities for you to get an understanding of recent cyber-crime developments as well as socialize with your InfoSec peers.

These meetings are also important because they offer you an opportunity to make personal contacts with law enforcement personnel. This connection gives you a great opportunity to ask questions and use these resources as a sort of "sounding board." I have had FBI agents present at a couple of my annual CIRP tests. As an InfoSec person, I can talk forever about cyber-threats during my annual CIRP tests, but I'm not sure it always sinks in. But when an FBI or USSS agent provides this information, it carries more weight. Another benefit of having the FBI or USSS agent at your annual CIRP test is to discuss with your CIRP team what is required to be a "Good Victim." Law Enforcement has various priorities and requirements that need to be met prior to assisting you with your crisis. It is naive to assume that they will be immediately accessible and willing/able to respond to your cyber-crisis if you are unprepared.

Using Plans to Augment Your Current ERM Efforts

As companies begin to embrace enterprise risk management (ERM) and develop a greater risk consciousness, the development of CIRPs will yield benefits for addressing risk(s). This applies not only to computer or IT risks; the benefits of a socialized, normalized, and documented plan that addresses a specific risk can have tremendous benefits for the organization.

Again, a plan is more than just a product in and of itself. It is a process. It is a mindset that can be applied to identifying resources, temporary organizational structures, controls and reporting mechanisms, contractual and statutory obligations, and other factors for a certain category of risk. Also, as you exercise this effort, you gain tremendous insight to a broader vision of what the corporation is and what risks the corporation needs to address.

I believe that, ultimately, this type of planning should become part of an organization's overall enterprise risk management effort. Since not all risks are preventable, or the prevention of a certain risk may not be cost-effective, often the best that the organization can hope for in the case of a low probability, high impact event is that there is sufficient due diligence to respond immediately to the incident and minimize the impact.

Writing Your Computer Incident Response Plan

I've spent a fair amount of time discussing cyber-crime, due diligence, crisis, and planning. Now it's time to pull up a chair and start writing your plan. As I explained earlier, Chapters 5 through 7 will review in detail a functioning data breach CIRP. Chapters 8 through 10 will do the same for a malware CIRP. In this chapter, you'll learn about some fundamentals that will start you down the road of writing a good CIRP. I'll provide examples for most of the topics discussed here in the chapters that follow.

What Problem Are You Solving?

First and foremost, before you commit any of your time to this effort, you need to consider what problem you are solving. What risk to the organization requires this effort? This will help you develop a scope of this risk and the ensuing effort required to respond to it. Who will be affected if this risk occurs, and what will be the impact if there is no response? You've already learned about requirements-based execution. What requirements are relevant to this risk or crisis? Are there laws regarding this crisis? You need to know enough about the problem to justify not only your time, but the time you will be asking of others to draft a CIRP.

Don't Bother if You Don't Have an Executive Sponsor

That's it. If the sponsor isn't at least a company vice president who is willing to *own* the plan and provide support, your efforts are likely doomed. The risk that you are addressing must carry a consequence to someone senior in the organization. If you are writing a data breach or a malware CIRP, either the chief information officer (CIO) or the chief information security officer (CISO)/chief security officer (CSO) should be involved. Not only does this person need to be aware of your efforts, but he or she must be willing to come to your aid when you run into roadblocks.

Most plans fail to materialize because of lack of executive support. Many of the people you will need to reach out to in order to develop this plan have competing priorities. Your executive sponsor's political "horse-power" or "juice" may be needed down the road. If you are unable to find an executive sponsor, you need to seriously question the value of the plan you are writing.

Using an Advisory Committee: My Plan vs. Our Plan

Before you begin writing, you should determine who will be involved in responding to the crisis you intend to address and ask them to sit on an advisory committee. This committee won't write the plan (that's still your job), but they will meet once a month for no more than 90 minutes. Their sole task is to review your efforts to date. They can ask questions. If you are lucky, they will provide guidance and be active participants. At a minimum, you need to provide them the opportunity to criticize the plan before it becomes "official."

In the "Preface" of the two plans detailed in the book, you will see that I take the opportunity to recognize and thank the members of my advisory committees. Especially if the crisis has corporate consequences, the members of this committee should extend well beyond the boundaries of IT. Recognizing advisory board members in the plan serves multiple purposes. First, it shows the reader that this is a "corporate" plan that is supported by multiple stakeholders, not just your plan or IT's plan. It also shows the reader the breadth of corporate perspective involved in developing the plan. And it ensures that the CIRP is fully socialized and normalized within the organization.

I engaged my advisory committee in a way that required the least amount of their time. Many of these people play significant roles within the company and their time is limited. I always approached them with the commitment that I would do my best to limit their efforts. I provided a brief synopsis of my efforts from the previous month no less than a week prior to the meeting. I asked all of them to read the notes prior to the meeting, as I would not be reviewing them during the meeting. During the meeting, I solicited comments, and attendees usually had comments. I had a couple of meetings where there we no comments. Those meetings lasted no more than 5 minutes. These folks didn't get to where they are in the organization by not doing their homework. If things were heading on the right track, or the efforts I presented weren't relevant to them, I respected their time by ending the meeting promptly. The best meetings, however, were those in which comments were plentiful. I welcomed these suggestions, because it was an opportunity for me to learn more about their roles and perspectives and ultimately to follow through on the premise that we were there to develop a thorough plan that would serve the entire corporation and not just IT. Again, this wasn't my plan we were discussing; it was "our" plan.

Understanding Your Audiences

Before you start writing the CIRP, you need to consider the various audiences that will read the plan. Although the title of this book is *Computer Incident Response Planning*, you are actually planning a *corporate* response to an IT risk. You need to start writing the plan assuming that it will have a broad audience. Some will read the plan prior to it ever being used. InfoSec/IT management will read it to ensure that it is sufficient to mitigate the risks for which they are responsible. Individuals who are designated to play an active role in the CIRP will also read it. (You hope!) Folks at the tactical level may wonder what will be their role; at the technical level, folks will evaluate the plan for technical accuracy and its efficacy for their specific technology interests. Managers at the operational level should also review the plan to see how it will impact their organizations and potentially their roles during times of crisis.

People outside of IT will need to review the CIRP. Depending on the risk being addressed, folks from legal, public affairs, corporate security, insurance, cash management, internal audit, compliance—you name it—will read the plan. If the CIRP deals with Payment Card Industry (PCI), a PCI auditor will review the plan.

If you actually have a serious incident, you can bet that senior leadership within the corporation will be looking at the plan, hoping that you developed an effective mechanism to address the crisis. If you have to reach outside of your organization, whether to law enforcement, third-party consultants, or your acquiring bank(s) (for a PCI data breach), all of these folks are a potential audience for the plan. Make sure the plan is technically accurate but simple enough that a CEO can understand it. Most folks don't need to understand the various components in detail, but they need to be assured that you have performed the necessary anticipation, collaboration, and research to produce an effective CIRP. You should avoid being verbose, but you must ensure that sufficient narrative is included to communicate effectively to all these different audiences.

Leveraging the Table of Contents

The idea of sitting down and writing anything can be daunting. Writing this book seemed like a monumental task—until I got started. I took the same approach for this book that I did for both of the CIRPs: I started with a table of contents. Start with top-level topics and define the basic framework of the plan. I referred to the NIST (National Institute of Standards and Technology) "Computer Security Incident Handling Guide - Special Publication 800-61" for an idea of how I should organize the plan.

To start my CIRPs, I list the major areas of the plan and designate them as "Heading 1" style in a Microsoft Word document. Then for each of those sections, use the "Heading 2" style for subtopics. Some areas went all the way down through four layers ("Heading 4") of the outline.

Specific examples of the two plans are included in Chapters 5–10. What follows is a brief discussion of some suggested sections that could make up the outline or framework of your plan. Remember that your plan needs to address your unique requirements.

Plan Introduction

I start every plan with a foreword, where I set the tone of the plan and recognize the members of my advisory committee. This is the first thing that anybody reading the plan will see and an opportunity to instill confidence in the reader.

As part of the introduction, I recommend a brief discussion on the following topics (again, later chapters provide specific examples):

▶ **Objective**   A statement of the "five W's" (who, what, when, where, and why) for the plan. I ultimately want the objective to relate all the way up to the business: what benefits to the business/organization are provided with this plan? This is one of the first things people see when they read the plan.

▶ **Scope**   What this plan covers, and what it doesn't cover.

▶ **Assumptions**   Helps the reader better understand the limitations of the plan.

▶ **Ownership**   More of a formality in which you identify the executive(s) responsible for the plan and how to contact them. I usually put my name and contact info somewhere below, since any concerns regarding the plan will ultimately roll down to me.

▶ **Execution and command topologies**   Pictures are worth a thousand words. They help the reader visualize both how the plan itself is organized and how the actual execution of the plan will look from an organizational perspective. You'll see these in the following chapters when I focus on the two actionable plans. Remember that senior executives like pictures.

▶ **Plan structure**   Your plan will contain a significant amount of information, and all of that information has to be managed. Some is perishable (such as point of contact listing) and needs to be maintained constantly, and some of it is owned and maintained by external parties. Ultimately, the information you use as part of your plan must be reasonably current in order for it to be relevant. At a minimum, you should know at time of crisis the currency of the information that you are using. You will see examples of this with both of the plans detailed in later chapters.

Again, the plan introduction section is really about the plan itself.

Incident Preparation

This section is about preparing to respond to crisis. Here's a mental exercise that I have used: I have a crystal ball, and I know that in three weeks we will have an incident. What can we do now to prepare for this incident?

I've already talked about *requirements-driven execution*. This is where you manage the various requirements you will need to meet. Data breach laws are a good example: in this part of the plan, you can provide details on the requirements of all the applicable laws.

.If this plan were to be used in three weeks, what kind of information would you need to share with others? How about data flow diagrams? And a summary of all the logging you do? This information could be very helpful for third-party resources or law enforcement.

If you lose PCI or personally identifiable information (PII) data, you will probably need to provide some sort of notification to affected parties. You may want to research who in your organization or in your community can help you send out all those letters.

How about credit monitoring? You will need to have some idea of who offers that service and their costs. Depending on the risk you are addressing, this is the section of the plan where anticipation and research can really pay off when it is time to respond.

In the case of a malware outbreak plan, this is a great place to introduce a containment strategy and a business impact analysis of using those "choke points" you've identified to contain an outbreak.

If you had to put together a set of documents needed to respond to a crisis, this is where they would be listed. Again, all of this info is included in the plans discussed later in the book.

Incident Detection, Analysis, and Declaration

At some point, you *will* have an incident. In this section of the plan, you detail the various sources of information that will enable you to detect that you are in a crisis situation. You also should detail exactly what constitutes an incident in this section.

A tremendous gap exists between *suspicious events* or *alerts* and an actual *incident*. Also, the IT definition might not be the same as that of corporate legal. This is where that socialization and normalization manifest, and it's where you compile and document a cohesive, "corporate" description of an *incident.*

You will also perform the necessary technical and business analysis to determine the severity of the crisis. It is critical that these definitions be documented and reviewed throughout the organization and not just by IT or InfoSec.

Finally, at some point, you are going to have to make the determination that you have an incident and mobilize the needed resources to address it. Chapters 5 and 7 will give you a better idea of the details required for this section of your plan.

Incident Response

Based on the parameters that your organization has documented in your CIRP, you've mobilized resources to address an emerging crisis. Now what? This is the section of the plan where you detail "who does what when." You will most likely need to establish an ad hoc organization to deal with this crisis. You will need to establish a decision-making structure so that decisions can be made and friction resolved. A "battle rhythm" should be laid out in your plan so everyone responding knows what's expected of him or her while ensuring that all your time isn't spent trying to make decisions at the cost of the time necessary to execute. Your plan should prescribe the various roles that need to be filled so there can be a "division of labor" sufficient to address the risk. You will need to address both technical considerations as well as administrative concerns. Although technical SMEs are working with your technology, public affairs, legal, and all those non-IT folks will also need to address the numerous other obligations your organization now faces.

Finally, at some point, you will have to declare an end to the incident. Hopefully your plan will have invested some time in determining a shared definition of when you can terminate the incident response.

Plan Maintenance/Post Incident

A number of post incident and maintenance issues are required to keep your plan up to date so that it is relevant during time of crisis. This is also a good place to discuss learning from your efforts. Whether your organization calls them "lessons learned," "after action," or "post mortem," a good CIRP is based on continuous learning and improvement, because everything is constantly changing. You should also mention here that it's a good idea to test your plan on at least an annual basis.

Development of an Ad Hoc Organization to Respond to Crisis

One of the most significant values a CIRP brings to the organization is the ability to mobilize your resources for this low probability–high impact event. If this risk you are addressing is a high probability event, you should probably structure your day-to-day organization to respond to it. If it is a low probability that may never happen to your organization, it makes sense to have this ad hoc structure ready to implement during time of crisis.

Developing this organization requires an understanding of several things. The most important is an understanding of what critical internal and external requirements the organization needs to fulfill. This is also a good opportunity to develop an understanding of your organization's center of gravity. The U.S. Department of Homeland Security (DHS) in its National Infrastructure Protection Plan (NIPP) defines risk as a vulnerability coupled with a threat that creates a consequence:

$$Risk = Vulnerability + Threat + Consequence$$

This idea of consequence is critical for you to understand. The objective of your plan is to mitigate undesirable consequences to your organization. You need to make sure that you can protect your organization's Center of Gravity. Your next step is to identify the various resources needed to respond to this crisis. These may be either internal or external resources. Next, develop a hierarchy that empowers a singular leadership entity, either an individual or a committee. I call mine the "Incident Commander" because of my military background.

The next component of the hierarchy is the submanagers, who, working for the "incident commander," will get the work done to mitigate the risk. You have two opposing concerns to address when you're determining how you will organize the response team. One concern is this idea of division of labor. You need to spread out the work sufficiently so that tasks can be performed and managed in parallel and in relatively short order during a crisis. The opposing concern is that you organize these resources in a way that makes sense of their individual and collective capabilities. Simply put, you will want all the technical folks in one group working for a technical manager. Or, if the response is predominantly a technical response, you may want to aggregate like technologies or like roles. Whenever possible, utilize the existing organizational structures within the day-to-day organization.

Plan Development:
Data Breach

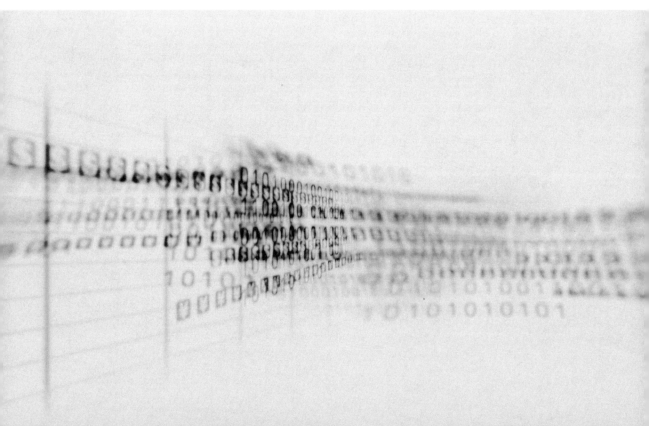

CHAPTER

5

Your Data Breach CIRP: Incident Preparation

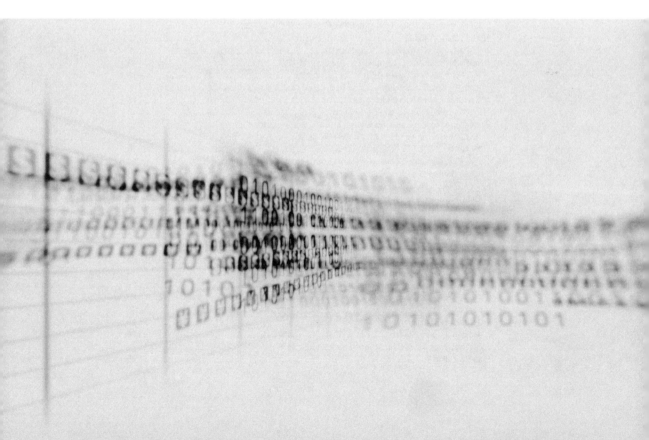

I n the next six chapters, we will dissect two existing CIRPs. Text that represents content taken directly from active, living plans is formatted differently from regular descriptive text. Some of this information may be redundant with information presented in previous chapters.

After your cover page, your plan should include a table of contents that presents the framework of the plan. Also, depending on the size of the plan, the TOC provides a helpful tool for readers to zoom in on the material they are most interested in.

Listed here is the table of contents, for the "Data Breach Plan":

If, after reading Chapter 3, you found yourself scratching your head and thinking, "There's no way I am going to be able to build a framework in my table of contents," feel free to start with this one and adjust it to meet your specific needs. The idea is that the "Heading 1" items are the major sections of the plan and all the subsequent headings support the major sections.

The TOC is followed by the revision history, which is a standard requirement for most corporate documents.

The foreword is next, and is, in my opinion, one of the most important sections I want my new reader to see:

Foreword

A Plan Is Preparation Manifested

This document has been written to meet the PCI DSS requirement for an immediately executable incident response plan. However, sound Information Security Management principles suggest that all organizations entrusted to maintain the Confidentiality, Integrity, and

Availability of sensitive data should incorporate Protective, Detective, and Corrective measures to ensure such a result. Planning is a corrective mechanism and should be part of any Information Security effort. For planning to be an effective, corrective mechanism, it must provide a solid foundation as to its execution, specific information so that participants are empowered with current and relevant knowledge, and yet it must be broad as to not constrict an organization's ability to respond to unforeseen events. Planning will rarely answer all the questions that come up during an incident, but it should provide a repository of thoughtful anticipation, collaboration, and research. Furthermore, to assure a plan's continued usefulness, it should be tested and updated on a regular basis. A plan's true value is measured by the relevance of the information and processes it provides at a time of crisis.

XYZ Information Security is grateful to the following individuals who participated as part of the CIRP Advisory Committee and provided valuable insight into the development of this plan:

Bill Jones and Ray Jones – XYZ Corporate Counsel
Al Jones – XYZ Information Technology Compliance Office
Diana Jones –XYZ IT Retail Portfolio Management
Raj Jones – Security Consultant
Scott Jones – XYZ IT Audit
John Jones – XYZ Corporate Loss Prevention
Tom Jones – XYZ Corporate Communications
Claire Jones – XYZ Marketing
Pat Jones and Pam Jones – XYZ Disaster Recovery

As I mentioned in previous chapters, your foreword sets both the tone of the plan and it also details to the reader all the different perspectives that contributed to this plan. If you staff your advisory committee well, the reader will see that you have done your best to address all the various requirements of the organization.

The next section of the CIRP is the "Plan Introduction," which details the various nuances of the plan itself. The first item is the "Plan Objective."

Plan Introduction

Plan Objective

A collaboratively developed, documented, and validated plan that enables XYZ to immediately respond to a data compromise in a manner that demonstrates appropriate Due Diligence in order to protect the integrity of our systems, defend against potential litigation, maintain confidence in the XYZ brand, and ultimately preserve shareholder value and customer privacy.

Your plan's objective should link your efforts with the benefits it provides to the organization. This is important because it justifies the time and effort that was spent developing this plan. You should also develop an idea of the plan's objectives and its value proposition prior to reaching out to the members of the advisory committee.

The next component is the "Plan Scope and Assumptions." It sets the expectations of the reader and details the boundaries of the plan.

Plan Scope and Assumptions

The scope of this Computer Incident Response Plan (CIRP) is to provide corrective actions for Data Compromises involving primarily PCI data.
The following assumptions are applicable to this plan:

1. Only one data compromise has occurred.
2. External parties are not initially involved (law enforcement, and so on).
3. The plan will be developed based on a worst-case scenario such as the T.J.Maxx scope of data compromise.
4. Plan will allow for maximum flexibility in the event of a "Priority 2" event allowing for the lowest level of management involvement whenever possible.
5. This plan will be a living document, subject to regular updates and testing.

The next section assists the reader in conceptualizing how the plan and the ad hoc CIRP team are organized. The idea is that before they start to read their way into the details of the plan, they have a bird's eye view of both the plan and the execution organization.

Plan Execution and Command Topologies

This plan is based on the following topology:

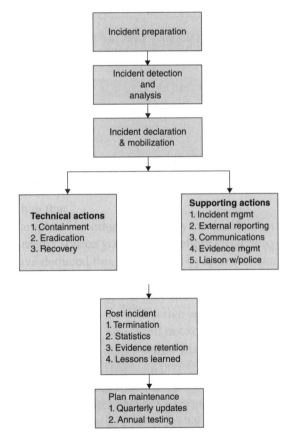

This topology illustrates that the technical tasks of Containment, Eradication, and Recovery should be considered in parallel with the necessary Supporting Actions.

Incident Command must also accommodate the execution topology. In large events, it may not be feasible to have all the various participants directly interfacing during the execution of the plan. A management hierarchy may become necessary to facilitate a more efficient level of command and control for a large Data Compromise incident.

The following topology should be followed for managing a data compromise incident:

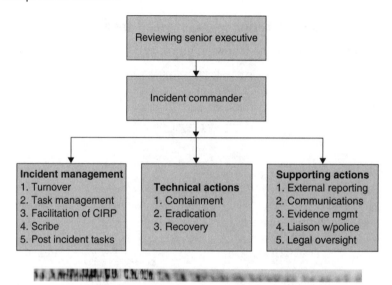

Greater discussion of these topologies will be discussed in Chapter 6.

The next section lists the plan's executive "owner." This section serves as a point of contact if there are questions or issues with the plan and also provides a little organizational "juice" as to who in management believes this is an important plan. I also include my contact info since any efforts regarding the plan will be assigned to me.

The XYZ CISO (Suzy Queue) is the senior executive responsible for the development, maintenance, and execution of this plan.

This plan is managed by the Information Security Operations Center (ISOC).

The ISOC Plans Point of Contact (POC) is

N McCarthy
1 Busy Street
Northern, CA 94500
(925) 123-4567

The next section of the plan introduction is the first instance of actionable content. By *actionable content*, I mean that this portion of the plan will need to be constantly updated and can have a significant impact on the relevance of your plan. It's called "Plan Structure" (which may not be the best term) and it is the section of the plan where we identify and manage all the various pieces of information that are used within the plan. I structure this section to be similar to how the military manages the various contents of their plans. Your plan will depend on many different types of information in order to be successful, and this is where that information is located.

Plan Structure

This plan is specifically designed for a data compromise incident. Contained within this plan are the following:

► **References**   References are both internal and external formal documents that contain information pertinent to the successful execution of the XYZ CIRP.

► **Enclosures**   Enclosures are typically informal documents that contain useful information, such as diagrams, spreadsheets, and so on. Enclosures are usually information relevant to the task at hand but not maintained or controlled by the author of this plan.

► **Tabs**   Tabs are specific items of information, relevant to the plan, but containing perishable data for which there is no other source. Tabs may typically include information such as Point of Contact data. Tab data will be located both within the text of the plan to support the flow of the document and in the Appendix for quick access.

► **Restricted information**   Restricted information is required for the execution of this plan and could be used by unauthorized individuals to the detriment of XYZ or its customers. References to restricted data in this document must be identified as such and will normally contain a link to the internal XYZShareIT site and will be password protected. Access to restricted information will be managed by the ISOC.

► **Hyperlinked**   All referenced materials that are available will be stored on the ShareIT (internal collaboration/file sharing) site with the CIRP and hyperlinked within the document. If the CIRP needs to be sent to third parties (without network access to the linked documents), an electronic copy will need to be created so that all offline documents will need to be included into the "offline" CIRP.

Updating and Synchronization

The information contained within this plan is valuable only as long as it is relevant. The objective of maintaining current information in a plan is to ensure that at time of execution, the plan provides relevant information to ensure successful execution. To this end, it is incumbent upon those tasked with maintaining this plan to confirm the currency of the references, enclosures, and tabs listed below.

Document	Last Verification	Responsible Party
Ref (1) NIST Guide	2/25/11	ISOC
Ref (2) DHS NIPP	2/25/11	ISOC
Ref (3) DOJ Handbook	2/25/11	ISOC
Ref (4) XYZ Crisis Communications SOP	3/23/11	Corp Public Affairs
Ref (5) CSO Magazine Article on Data Compromise Notification Letters	N/A	N/A
Ref (6) XYZ Malware Mitigation SOP	5/19/11	Field Services
Ref (7) VISA Procedure	2/25/09	Compliance
Ref (8) XYZ Digital Evidence Verification	5/30/10	XYZ Forensics
Ref (9) XYZ Digital Evidence Chain of Custody Procedure	5/30/10	XYZ Forensics
Ref (10) Third Party Security PFI Services Scope of Work (SOW)	5/19/10	ISOC
Encl (1) PCI Data flow	5/30/10	Compliance
Encl (2) Web posting by Hannaford CEO	N/A	N/A
Encl (3) XYZ Mutual Nondisclosure Agreement	3/23/12	Vendor Mgmt Office
Tab (A) Compliance and Statutory Framework Document	5/30/8	Compliance
Tab (B) ISOC Threat Portfolio	3/22/12	ISOC
Tab (C) PCI Log Data Retention	1/1/12	ISOC
Tab (D) Third Party Connections	11/4/11	ISOC
Tab (E) Sample Data Compromise Notification letters	N/A	ISOC

Document	Last Verification	Responsible Party
Tab (F) ISOC Monitoring Feeds Summary	5/30/11	ISOC
Tab (G) Incident Notification POCs	5/19/11	ISOC
Tab (H) Key Resource Escalation/Back-up Instruction	5/30/11	ISOC
Tab (I) Law Enforcement Points of Contact (POC)	5/19/11	Loss Prevention
Tab (J) CIRP SWAT Management Checklist	1/14/12	ISOC
Tab (K) Disaster Recovery Summary	3/22/12	ISOC

This concludes the "Plan Introduction" section of the CIRP. Remember that this is simply an example. You may choose to include more or less content.

The next major section of the CIRP prepares us for execution of the CIRP. This section is called "Incident Preparation" and its goal is to act as a starting point for all the anticipation and research you have done. Anything that you can imagine needing during the crisis you are resolving should be included here. I also use this section to discuss in greater length the more significant references, enclosures, and tabs used as part of the plan. I will also hyperlink the materials within the narrative section whenever possible to my internal corporate site. There are some restrictions to "sensitive" documents.

Incident Preparation

The purpose of this section of the plan is to ensure that adequate information regarding the (PCI) environment at XYZ is immediately available in the event of a computer incident. This information should be verified on a regular basis to ensure its relevancy/accuracy.

Statutory/Compliance Framework

Compliance and Statutory Framework Document (Tab A) is maintained in the Appendix of this plan. This document outlines the various regulations and obligations with potential applicability to XYZ based on physical business locations and applicable HIPAA/SOX/PCI requirements. This document is for reference purposes only. Questions regarding applicability and interpretation of this material and other legal requirements should be routed through XYZ's corporate legal department.

Sensitive Data

PCI Data Map (Encl 1) **RESTRICTED**

PCI Data Flow Diagram (Enclosure 1) is a detailed map of credit card data flows within XYZ. This document is highly sensitive and confidential to XYZ and shall be designated "RESTRICTED." The disclosure of this document to unauthorized parties may cause serious risk or injury to XYZ. This document is maintained by Compliance and is included to provide involved parties a detailed understanding of the XYZ PCI environment. A link to a secure site with the file is maintained in the Appendix section of the plan.

ISOC Threat Portfolio (PCI) (Tab B) **RESTRICTED**

The ISOC maintains an application threat analysis for PCI applications (Tab B) as a subset of the ISOC Threat Portfolio. This document is highly sensitive and confidential to XYZ and shall be designated "RESTRICTED." The disclosure of this document to unauthorized parties may cause serious risk or injury to XYZ. This analysis is a collection of all exceptions, vulnerabilities, potential threats, and existing mitigations efforts for all of the PCI data sets. This document is maintained by the ISOC and is included to provide involved parties a detailed understanding of the XYZ Inc. PCI environment. A link to a secure site with this file is maintained in the Appendix section of the plan.

PCI Log Data (Tab C)

Per Section 10 of the PCI DSS, XYZ logs all events pertaining to PCI systems. This tab details the SYSLOG (system logging) data and points of contact for all PCI logging.

Third-Party (Payment) Connections (Tab D)

XYZ has a number of third-party connections for various services. The pre-paid card connections include FTP with SSL, HTTPS, or leased line connections. Listed in this tab are the third-party connections carrying PCI data and their specific POCs within XYZ.

The next area of anticipation revolves around the use of third-party services to support the CIRP. In the context of this plan, third-party services also include XYZ corporate resources that aren't normally associated with IT or InfoSec.

Third-Party Services

In the event of a data compromise, specific third-party services should be necessary to meet either contractual or statutory requirements imposed on XYZ. The section below is an effort to anticipate and identify those third-party activities.

PCI Forensic Investigator (PFI)

Third-Party Security Inc. has been contracted to provide immediate on-site PFI support in the event of a data breach. XYZ has pre-paid for a week of support. The annual contract also contains other support provisions and can be accessed at the following link: XYZ.Internal.site.

To declare an emergency with Third-Party Security, call 888-123-4567 and mention that you are with XYZ. XYZ's assigned Incident Response analyst is Michael Jones. He can be reached at 123-456-7890 and his e-mail is Michael.Jones@Fake SecuritycompanyURL.com.

Identity Protection Services
Road Crossings Inc.

This vendor has been used by XYZ in previous data compromises.

Road Crossings offer affected parties twelve months of web-based Identity Protection services from one credit bureau. Within their standard offering is Identity Theft Insurance, Credit Education Specialist, and an Identity Theft Recovery Unit.

Set-up fee is $2500 and $30 for each affected party that actually enrolls with the service. Previous enrollment is approximately 20% of affected individuals. The Road Crossings notification template letter is listed below in the Appendix as "Sample Data Compromise Notification letters (Tab E)." Road Crossings will provide unique access codes for each affected party. This access code must be included in the notification letter.

Road Crossings POC:

Katherine Jones
Dir, Enterprise Solutions
703-123-4567
KJones@RoadCrossings.com

or

Melissa Jones
Sr. Marketing Assoc
703-123-7890
MJones@RoadCrossings.com

HailMary

HailMary is a competitor to Road Crossings and has not been used previously by XYZ. HailMary is a better known brand and provides additional services listed below. Their sample notification letter is listed below in the Appendix as "Sample Data Compromise Notification letters (Tab E)."

HailMary current charges:

1–5000: $24/person
5001–15,000: $18/person
15,001-plus: $12/person
HailMary charges per person regardless of whether they sign up for the service.

HailMary POC:

Anthony Jones
Bus Development
480-457-1234
Anthony.Jones@HailMary.com

Assuming 20% of affected parties utilize identity protection services (based on previous XYZ experience); the break-even point between HailMary and Road Crossings is approximately 135 affected persons.

Please refer to Tab (E) for Sample Data Compromise Notification Letters, Reference (9) CSO Magazines Article on Data Breach Notification Letters, and the "Release of Public-Facing Documents" section of this plan prior to drafting any notification letters.

Compromise Notification Fulfillment

In the event of a data compromise, affected parties will often need to be notified. Previously, XYZ has mailed letters to each affected person.

Specific information regarding the contents of this letter is listed below in the Appendix as "Sample Data Compromise Notification letters Tab (E)."

All public-facing documents, prior to their release, should follow the process outlined in the "Release of Public-Facing Documents" section of this plan.

Listed below are resources that can provide the necessary support to merge affected party data into a letter template, print, fold, stuff, and mail the notification.

Initially a personalized letter will need to be created for each affected person. The mail merge function will require an Excel file with all data for the specific affected parties. This spreadsheet should include the following:

Name
Street Address
City
State
Zip Code
Access code for identity protection service provider.

This information will need to be merged with a letter template. Examples of such letters provided by the Identity Protection service (available below in the Appendix: "Sample Data Compromise Notification letters (Tab E)" and released as part of the "Release of Public-Facing Documents" section of this plan. It is recommended that the letter be formatted for a standard XYZ #10 window envelope

Once the affected party information is merged with the letter template, the letters will need to be printed, folded, stuffed into an envelope, and mailed.

XYZ internal resources for less than 1000 letters:

Mail Merge:
Primary: Elaine Jones, HR Development – (925) 789-1234 or Elaine.Jones@XYZ.com
Secondary: Linda Jones, HR Development – (925) 789-1234 or Linda.Jones@XYZ.com.
The fulfillment process (print, fold, stuff, mail) can be performed by
Primary: Sherman Jones, Duplication Services – (925) 789-3456 or Sherman.Jones@XYZ.com
Secondary: Maryann Jones, Corporate Printing Services – (925) 789-0987 or Maryann.Jones@XYZ.com.

For situations requiring 1000 or more letters, a third-party vendor with previous service to XYZ has been listed below.

Black Ink Printing has done mass mailings for XYZ for the past several years.

Black Ink Printing contact information:

123 Muni Court
Northern, CA 94500
(925) 567-1234, voice
(925) 567-3456 fax
Contact person: Gary Jones, Mailing Dept Manager, ext 107
Alternate contact person: Curtis Jones, Vice President, ext 111

Maximum* cost for above services (ref: estimate #33668, First Class postage not included):

► 1–249 letters: Minimum $460

► 250–999 letters: $1.85 each

► 1000–9999 letters: $0.56 each

► 10,000–49,999 letters: $0.18 each

► 50,000 and more: $0.13 each

* Cost may be lower, based on quantity

Items needed from XYZ:

► One page letter in Microsoft Word format.

► Excel file with names and addresses.

► #10 window envelopes (Black Ink Printing can print and supply if needed).

► After data is processed, XYZ will receive a postage request from MyCousin Vinnie. Postage check must be received by Black Ink Printing before letters are mailed. Check is made payable to Postmaster.

Black Ink Printing and Mailing, Inc., will perform the following services:

► Process and prepare the data to United States Postal Service Specifications.

► Pre-sort the addresses for discounted First Class postage rates.

► Email XYZ a postage request.

► Merge the names and addresses onto the notification letter.

► Print the letter (all black ink, one side) on 24# white paper.

► Fold the letter and insert it into a XYZ #10 window envelope.

- ▶ Inkjet our postal permit imprint (indicia) on the XYZ envelope.
- ▶ Estimated production time for these services:
  - ▶ Up to 1000 letters: 2 days.
  - ▶ Up to 25,000 letters: 3 days.
  - ▶ Up to 50,000 letters: 4 days.
  - ▶ Up to 100,000 letters: 6 days.
- ▶ Prepare necessary postal documents and deposit mail at the US post office.

Prior to using services from Blank Ink Printing, a current NDA needs to be in place.

The next section of the "Incident Preparation" section is the subsection "Incident Detection, Analysis, and Declaration." You just don't go out and declare an incident whenever you feel like it; never mind the whole "boy who cried wolf" story. You have put a fair amount of effort into this plan so far, and you don't want to spoil it because you didn't prepare for that phase of time leading up to when you actually act upon your CIRP. The first thing you must do is understand and document how you expect to be notified that you actually have a suspected incident. Documenting this process has implications on how others within the corporation work with you and how your internal InfoSec (ISOC) operates as well. Here is an example of the "Sources of Precursors and Indicators" subsection of the "Incident Detection, Analysis and Declaration" section.

Sources of Precursors and Indicators

Listed below are potential sources of data compromise detection available to XYZ:

ISOC Monitoring Feeds Tab (F) (XYZ RESTRICTED)

The ISOC Monitoring Feeds (Tab F) is a detailed listing of the current ISOC monitoring feeds within XYZ. This document is XYZ Restricted. The disclosure of this document to unauthorized parties may cause serious risk to XYZ. This document is maintained by the ISOC as part of its day-to-day responsibilities. It is included within the plan to provide a detailed understanding of the various sources of monitoring input available to the ISOC and parties involved in investigating a data compromise.

Malware

On any given day, malicious programs such as viruses, spyware, Trojan horses, and so on (collectively referred to as "malware" for this document), will disrupt someone's productivity. Many of us have heard of the impact viruses can have on business productivity. We should also be aware of the pervasive nature of "spyware." These programs load onto your PC and collect sensitive information such as keystrokes and transmit them back to some outside entity. Although most malware incidents are benign, malware should be of a concern for all of us because it has the potential not only to disrupt our daily activities, but in some instances, malware can be an effective tool to steal both personal and corporate information that can be used by others to our detriment. Malware can also be an effective tool for gaining and maintaining unauthorized access into the XYZ IT infrastructure. Because the malware threat is so pervasive and dynamic, the ability of an organization to deal with this threat effectively is extremely challenging. The ISOC, Desktop Services, and Field Services have promulgated the XYZ Malware Mitigation Process. This Standard Operating Procedure (SOP) makes first responders aware that malware can be used as a tool to penetrate the XYZ network and defines specific steps that are to be taken should an occurrence of malware be identified as being a threat to XYZ. As part of this process, the ISOC is identified as the lead investigative entity in the event malware is identified as being part of an attempted/successful penetration of the XYZ environment. As such, this malware process may provide an indication that the network has been or is in the process of being breached.

Law Enforcement, Common Point of Purchase (CPP), or Other External Sources

The company is made aware of a suspected or confirmed data compromise in the following ways:

▶ Via customer complaint (suspected)

▶ Via bank (merchant services) (suspected)

▶ By law enforcement (suspected)

▶ By Corp Security/loss prevention (LP) monitoring & investigations

Network Operations Center (NOC), Service Desk, and Other Internal Sources of Detection

It is not always obvious when a data compromise has occurred. Often other anomalies within the enterprise can serve as possible indicators of a compromise. Activities such as unusual network traffic, malware, and other questionable activity may be suspect and should be taken seriously. Whenever these types of incidents/tickets become known by other support entities within XYZ, the ISOC should be contacted so a thorough investigation of a data compromise can occur.

VISA lists the following as signs that your system may have been compromised:

- ▶ Unknown or unexpected outgoing Internet traffic from the cardholder environment
- ▶ Presence of unexpected IP (Internet Protocol) addresses on store or wireless networks
- ▶ Unknown or unexpected network traffic from store and headquarter locations
- ▶ Unknown or unexpected services and applications configured to launch automatically on system boot
- ▶ Anti-virus programs malfunctioning or becoming disabled for unknown reasons
- ▶ Failed login attempts in system authentication and event logs
- ▶ Vendor or third-party connections to the card holder environment without prior consent and/or a trouble ticket
- ▶ SQL injection attempts in the web server event logs
- ▶ Authentication event log modifications (such as unexplained event logs being deleted)
- ▶ Suspicious after-hours file system activity (such as user login or activity to POS server after hours)
- ▶ Presence of .zip, .rar, .tar, and other types of unidentified compressed files potentially containing cardholder data

XYZ Corporation 800 Fraud / Ethics Hotline

Another source to detect possible inappropriate cyber-activity (and possible insider breach) is the company's ethics hotline. XYZ's ethics hotline is 866-234-1234 and is staffed during normal business hours by Corporate Loss Prevention. Robert Jones is the primary point of contact and typically answers the hotline. He has been advised to contact Information Security in the event of reported activities involving inappropriate cyber-activity.

The next topic we need to cover is what really defines an incident. If you listen to all the IT vendors out there, they would lead you to believe that their technology is so good that when you get their "You've been breached!" alert you are good to go. That is simply not the case. There are so many different security events that come across the network. Talk about "Fog of War," the vast majority are false positives or inconclusive. Documenting a shared definition of what defines a breach is critical to your plan. Also, when you are investigating some security events or other indicator of possible crisis, you should make sure that your analysis process is thorough—not just technically thorough, but thorough in the sense that you are asking the right organizational questions not just the IT ones.

Incident Thresholds

Not all losses of information constitute a data compromise. It is important prior to declaring a computer incident that you perform an analysis of the type of data affected and the circumstances of the alleged compromise. The thresholds provided below provide sufficient guidelines to classify both the necessary elements that constitute "data" and a "compromise."

Data Threshold

PCI

The Payment Card Industry (PCI) defines the following items as cardholder data. The loss of this type of information, if it meets the compromise criteria, would necessitate opening an "incident":

- ▶ Full magnetic-stripe data (such as tracks 1 and 2)
- ▶ Primary account number (PAN) with or without additional information such as PIN, CVV2, expiration date

PII

Current statutes applicable to XYZ define the following as sensitive personally identifiable information (PII) mandating follow-up actions. If this information becomes immediately identifiable to a specific person or (persons), an "incident" has occurred:

- ▶ Social Security number
- ▶ Credit card number

▶ Drivers license number

▶ State identification number

▶ Financial account number

▶ Non-public medical information

Compromise Threshold

PCI

VISA defines a compromise as follows: "deliberate electronic attacks on the communications or information processing systems, whether initiated by a disgruntled employee, a malicious competitor, or a misguided hacker.... Intrusion into computer system where unauthorized disclosure, modification, or destruction of cardholder data is suspected."

PII

XYZ has defined a compromise as the loss of control of PII data regardless of the media, including paper reports. Encrypted data is exempt from this threshold.

Incident Analysis

The initial impact analysis of a data compromise is an essential task in order to mobilize the appropriate technical and business resources effectively. Impact analysis also helps provide an initial estimation as to the scope of the data compromise. When determining the initial impact of a suspected compromise, it may not be possible to have all the necessary information prior to making an impact determination. It is critical during any assessment of potential impact not only to identify the source and credibility of the information you are using to determine impact, but also to admit the lack of certain relevant information.

Technical Impact

The technical impact analysis is where the scope of the data compromise is identified to specific data storage, processing, and transportation technologies. The more detail the better. Version numbers, IP addresses, and so on, are beneficial when identifying the necessary resources that need to be mobilized.

At a minimum, the technical impact analysis should contain answers to the following:

▶ What system(s) have been affected?

▶ What data has been compromised?

▶ What level of privilege did the attackers gain?

▶ How did the attackers gain access?

▶ What (if any) vulnerability was exploited?

▶ How widespread is that vulnerability within XYZ?

▶ Where we able to detect this incident?

▶ What component of the XYZ Information Security infrastructure failed to prevent/detect this attack?

Business Impact

Consider the following questions:

▶ Is public safety affected?

▶ How many customers may be affected by this incident?

▶ What products/goods/services does this compromise affect?

▶ Has XYZ lost the ability to control/record/measure/track any significant amount of inventory/products/cash/revenue?

▶ Is there any indication that this act would be exploited for malicious or criminal activity?

▶ Who currently knows about this incident (inside and outside of XYZ)?

At this point in time, you are reasonably sure you have an incident. The next step is to determine the scope of the response you need. To give you some background, this plan has been executed on an almost quarterly basis. Almost every quarter somebody loses some data. When we get notified, we go through this assessment process and, based on our answers, we determine whether it is a significant breach or a minor breach. In this plan, you will not see the terms "major" or "minor" as breach definitions. As part of the socialization process, when this plan was reviewed by Legal, there was some concern that use of the term "minor" could be a detriment to the corporation during post incident litigation. Imagine this: "Ladies and Gentlemen of the jury, the XYZ Corporation thought it was only a *minor* concern that my client(s) personal information was lost." These are the kinds of things you need to have considered when you put together your plan. Listed below are the criteria we developed between a Priority 1 and Priority 2 incident. (XYZ Corporation uses Priority 1 and Priority 2 terms as part of their IT production support processes. Priority 1 is a major incident.)

Incident Categories

As mentioned throughout this document, the scope of this plan is for the worst-case scenario in which significant information is lost. However, realizing that most of the compromises that do occur are unlikely to have such impact, the execution methodology of this plan is to start small and work up.

Incident categories play an important role in any executable plan because they provide a shared "measure" within the corporation of the size and potential impact of the data compromise. By defining incident categories, the organization is able to set expectations as to the severity and response actions necessary to deal with the situation. Thus, once the compromise is categorized, a shared understanding is possible within the organization. All initial incidents will be treated as Priority 2 until a decision is made by the CISO to declare a Priority 1 data compromise.

Priority 1

A Priority 1 data compromise is defined as an event that will have a significant impact on one or more of the following:

▶ The ability to provide products/goods/services to a significant number of customers

▶ The ability to control/record/measure/track/account for a significant amount of inventory/goods/revenue/cash/

▶ The unacceptable risk of significant punitive regulatory actions, contractual penalties, fraudulent criminal activity, and/or civil litigation

▶ Significant notoriety that has the potential to affect the stock price adversely, damage the brand, and/or cause widespread concern amongst customers/shareholders

A Priority 1 incident should be met with the full support of the corporation. As such, a Priority 1 incident may involve any or all of the following:

▶ Senior management involvement

▶ Several areas of due diligence on the part of XYZ including operational impact, criminal prosecution, contractual and statutory reporting, litigation preparation

- ▶ Unsolicited third-party involvement such as law enforcement, regulatory entities, civil subpoenas, and/or third-party contractual obligations
- ▶ Obligatory releases of internal information to the public, extensive media, and shareholder scrutiny

A Priority 1 incident declaration requires the approval of the CISO or their supervisor. A Priority 1 incident will initially impact all parties to this plan.

Priority 2

The most common type of data compromise that occurs is what most would characterize as a Priority 2 incident. For the execution of this plan, a Priority 2 incident is defined as follows:

- ▶ Does not fall within the description of a Priority 1 incident
- ▶ Subject to mandatory reporting or notification
- ▶ Requires due diligence by XYZ to assess, identify, and correct a deficiency within the organization's data processing, data usage, and/or information security infrastructure
- ▶ Presents the potential, but not the likelihood, of some sort of litigation and/or media attention

A Priority 2 incident response may not involve all components of this plan but should include the following:

- ▶ Execution at a level of management appropriate to address and resolve all issues raised
- ▶ A determination as to resources and functions required for resolution, as well as reports required
- ▶ Documentation of all efforts
- ▶ Management status reporting will be prepared and available if needed

Non-Actionable/Informational

XYZ Loss Prevention routinely deals with petty criminal acts that involve the theft of credit card data but do not fall within the requirements of PCI or statutory reporting. This type of event is normally considered to be a criminal act and is principally handled by Loss Prevention. Loss Prevention may work with law enforcement to coordinate effective responses to retail crime.

Loss Prevention reports such incidents to the following XYZ groups: Cash Management, InfoSec, Legal, and Retail Operations.

Now suppose you are ready to declare an incident. You have a reasonable belief that a breach has occurred. At a minimum, you should have sufficient evidence that the resources of the company need to be directed to investigate and if necessary resolve this crisis. This is a tough balance to maintain. You don't want to overreact and lose the confidence of the rest of the team, but if you wait too long for every last piece of information before mobilizing your CIRP, you may lose needed time and create a detriment to your response. That is the reason why my plan includes an e-mail format for a computer incident notification. This notification lets folks know that you are looking into a possible incident. This allows them an opportunity to prepare for a possible response and it gives you a little more breathing room as you continue to investigate your possible incident.

Here are a couple of thoughts on declaring an incident: I suggest that you stick to a consistent format with the messages you send out. You will see this in the next section. I also suggest that you be mindful that if they are in your environment stealing credit card numbers, they very well may also be reading your e-mail. If you suspect that you are dealing with an insider threat, or that your electronic communications may be compromised, then doing everything by phone may be the best way to go. This is just something to consider.

Incident Declaration

The formal declaration of a Data Compromise incident should not be taken lightly and will require the approval of a manager. A declaration of a "Priority 1 Data Compromise" will require the approval of the CISO or his/her designated backup. Accurate reporting in the initial stages of an incident is critical to ensure the proper mobilization of resources necessary to deal with the incident. When a data compromise is first suspected, an Initial Incident Notification message will be sent out to those members identified in the notification/mobilization listing below.

Incident Notification and Mobilization

Initial Incident Notification is the process of notifying relevant parties of a *possible* compromise that is currently under investigation. The initial notification should contain the following information:

COMPUTER INCIDENT NOTIFICATION
The parties listed below are investigating a *possible* data compromise:

Date/time:
Incident coordinator POC:

Approving manager POC:
Source of detection/notification:
Data compromised:
Compromise characteristics:
Encrypted data:
Technical impact:
Business impact:
Next Steps:
Confirmation/Denial of compromise:
Obstacles (if any):
Next update and Means:

Incident Declaration is the process of notifying relevant parties once a conclusion has been made that there is probable cause to believe that XYZ has been compromised. This declaration does not require complete knowledge of the circumstances of a compromise, but sufficient evidence that would cause a prudent person to believe a compromise has occurred. An incident declaration needs to contain the following information:

COMPUTER INCIDENT DECLARATION – Priority 1 /Priority 2
You are being notified that a DATA COMPROMISE HAS OCCURRED and XYZ resources will be required to support this incident.

Incident summary:
Priority 1 incident justification:
Technical impact:
Business impact:
Coordination conference call to be held at:
Date
Time
Call in number
Passcode

Incident coordinator POC:
Approving manager POC:

Refer to the following items for additional information:

► The initial Incident Notification is attached to provide more details regarding the incident and efforts prior to making this declaration.

▶ In order to access the XYZ Computer Incident Response Plan (CIRP), refer to the internal XYZShareIT site.

▶ Access to XYZ RESTRICTED documents pertaining to the CIRP are also on the ShareIT site but are password protected to pre-authorized parties. Contact the ISOC at InfoSec.Operations@XYZ.com in order to have your name added to the access roster.

Below are the minimum expectations as to incident notification and mobilization:

Function	POC	Initial Notification	Minor Mobilization	Major Mobilization
CISO	Charles Jones	Informed	Involved	Involved
Mgr ISOC	Armando Jones	Involved	Involved	Involved
CIRP lead	Trisha Jones	Involved	Involved	Involved
Legal	Bill Jones	Informed	Involved	Involved
XYZ Forensics	Frank Jones	Informed	Involved	Involved
Loss Prevention	John Jones	Informed	Informed	Involved
Compliance	Elwin Jones	Informed	Informed	Involved
XYZ - IT Operations	Cheryl Jones	Informed	Informed	Involved
Treasury/Cash Mgmt	Dennis Jones	Informed	Informed	Involved
Public Affairs	Brad Jones	As required	Informed	Involved
CIRP SWAT Team	See POC List	As required	As required	Involved
Investor relations	Mary Jones	As required	As required	Involved
IT Retail Portfolio	Diana Jones	As required	As required	Involved
Disaster Recovery	Freddie Jones	As required	As required	Involved
Corp Acctg (SOX)	Dennis Jones	As required	As required	Informed
Advertising	Kim Jones	As required	As required	Informed
HR	Michele Jones	As required	As required	Informed

Typically, all involved parties will need to be contacted directly. Informed parties can be listed as a primary or secondary recipient on an e-mail.

Non-Actionable/Informational incidents do not require immediate notification. An e-mail announcement is sufficient to notify the following XYZ groups: Cash Management, InfoSec, Corp Legal, and Retail Operations should be sufficient.

Incident Documentation

Documentation serves a key role in responding to any incident. The ability to capture, distribute, and store detailed information regarding the efforts made responding to an incident are key to an efficient response, lessons learned, and post-event concerns. All participants should maintain a detailed log/journal of time spent, actions taken, and additional involved parties starting from the initial notification/detection through the termination of the event. This information will be collected during the termination of the event.

I include the incident documentation at the end of this section because it's important to start keeping a journal of all the efforts, even those efforts leading up to an actual incident. At this point, we're convinced something is going on and we need to marshal resources to deal with this new crisis. Hopefully, you have prepared for this moment and you are ready to notify members of the CIRP team. This is when you realize just how important all that preparatory work you've done really is. The next chapter will walk us through the execution of the data breach CIRP.

CHAPTER 6

Your Data Breach CIRP:
Plan Execution

Welcome to crisis. Remember all those theories about crisis that we discussed in Chapter 1? Here is where you either dominate them or they dominate you.

Remember that this is merely an example of what I crafted. You are free to organize your response in any manner that you and your organization deem to be most appropriate. The key is that your plan must empower you to take and maintain the initiative.

This chapter discusses the actual execution of your data breach plan. It will detail the ad hoc organization and all the various roles within the CIRP team. This plan is very narrative; it has to be. Many of the folks you will be relying on to fill these roles may not be as well versed in the plan as they should. Remember that this entire plan is initially developed for a low probability event, and with the exception of an annual test, most folks won't see this plan except in time of crisis. This plan should serve as sort of a text book so that your participants can gain sufficient knowledge to "study up" so they can perform their roles effectively.

Let's take a look at the various roles for a data breach incident:

Plan Execution

No plan is ever perfect. However, at a time of heightened activity and anxiety, having a consistent expectation amongst diverse parties, each with unique perspectives but with a shared objective, is invaluable. One of the objectives of this CIRP is to establish that consistent expectation as to the method of how XYZ will respond to a data compromise. The first expectation will be describing the roles and organization of the various principals to the execution of this plan. The second section will discuss common activities during an incident and recommend a repeatable format for their execution.

Organization and Roles

During the execution of the CIRP, four components of the response will need to be performing simultaneously. First, there will need to be a command function, which is responsible for "getting things done." Command is acutely aware of the situation and makes timely decisions to guide the group to achieve the desired results. To resolve a data compromise, technical actions will be required of affected technologies. Supporting actions will deal with the numerous, often externally driven, tasks defined as part of the CIRP, and there is a role to facilitate the incident response itself. These are all necessary functions, occurring simultaneously in times of great stress and potential confusion. It is imperative that all involved in the CIRP understand what is expected of them and the other members of the team.

The descriptions provided here are for a Priority 1 (Major) incident, possibly involving numerous resources within XYZ. In the event of a Priority 2 (Minor) event, the roles provided may be combined/collapsed, but the same basic functions are required to execute the CIRP.

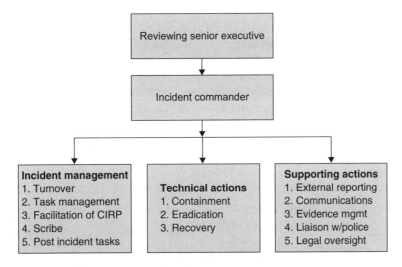

Incident Commander

The Incident Commander will ultimately be responsible for meeting the objective(s) of this plan. The Incident Commander must be empowered by the corporation to be capable of making timely decisions when necessary. During times of disagreement (friction), the Incident Commander will need to be formally apprised of the circumstances, presented with options, and he/she will need to determine the best course of action under the time constraints that are in effect. The Incident Commander must be apprised of the current efforts and will be responsible for status reports to senior management within XYZ.

Reviewing Senior Executive

It is important during a crisis that reasonably impartial management oversight is available to protect the interests of XYZ. By not being directly involved in the incident response, the Reviewing Senior Executive is able to remain informed yet emotionally detached. Secondly, with the Incident Commander busy with the immediate execution of the CIRP, the Reviewing Senior Executive can provide a common point of focus for other senior executives who may have concerns with the incident response. Finally, the Reviewing Senior Executive is best suited to determine if the current response is adequate and may direct additional resources, elevate the priority within XYZ, or direct more senior/capable leadership/resources to the task force.

Incident Management Coordinator

The Incident Management Coordinator is the "glue" the holds the CIRP execution together. Typically, the Incident Coordination Manager will be from the Information Security Operations Center (ISOC). Prior to the declaration of an incident, a number of actions are taken to prepare the plan, and to detect, analyze, and declare an incident. Upon the mobilization of the resources to respond to the incident, a turnover briefing will be necessary to bring all parties to the same level of understanding regarding both the compromise and the CIRP. During the execution of the CIRP, the Incident Management Coordinator will need to drive the execution of the plan. This includes the following functions:

► **Scribe** Keeps notes of all actions taken, discussions, and so on.
► **Task management** Tracks all deliverables assigned within the Data Compromise task force.
► **Facilitation of the CIRP** Ensures that all mechanisms of the CIRP are working as planned or changing as necessary. These include coordinating decision briefs and status briefs, setting up conference calls, and so on.
► **Post-incident tasks** Eventually, the incident will be terminated and a number of post-incident tasks will need to be accomplished to gain the full benefit of the execution of the plan.

The Incident Management Coordinator role will be performed by the manager of the ISOC.

Technical Actions Coordinator

Information resides on numerous platforms within XYZ. These platforms use different technologies and require specific subject matter expertise. The Technical Actions Coordinator is responsible for the containment, isolation, and recovery of the affected technical platforms. In the event of a Priority 1 compromise, where numerous technology platforms may be within the scope of the CIRP, the Technical Actions Coordinator provides the Incident Commander a singular focus for the technical actions within the plan.

Within the XYZ Corporation, the Incident Control Center (ICC) performs the role of coordinating technical resources to resolve production problems within the IT group. The ICC, as part of its day-to-day role, works with numerous application support groups, reports to management, and understands the importance of a coordinated response. In the event of a Priority 1 data compromise in which IT support will be required, the ICC will assume the role of the Technical Actions Coordinator. For Priority 2 compromises, the role of the ICC will need to be evaluated depending on the need for IT/platform/application support. The following participants within the CIRP should expect to fall under the Technical Actions Coordinator:

▶ (Data compromise) CIRP SWAT Team

▶ All affected IT application development and support groups

▶ IT infrastructure engineering and support groups

▶ Network security engineering group

▶ IT retail portfolio

▶ Disaster recovery

Supporting Actions Coordinator

A number of nontechnical issues must be addressed on behalf of the corporation in response to a data compromise. The role of the Supporting Actions Coordinator is to provide the Incident Commander a singular focus for this aspect of the plan. Tasks such as statutory and contractual reporting, evidence handling, liaison with outside entities (such as law enforcement [LE], acquiring banks) will be driven by the Supporting Actions Coordinator as part of the task force. The XYZ Compliance Group has a vested role in assuring that XYZ meets its obligation in such an incident. The Compliance Group is knowledgeable of the statutory and contractual obligations that need to be met in such an event. The Manager of the Compliance Group will serve as the Supporting Actions Coordinator in the event of a Priority 1 compromise. The following participants within the CIRP should expect to fall under the Supporting Actions Coordinator:

▶ Loss prevention

▶ Legal

- ▶ Forensics (InfoSec)
- ▶ Public affairs
- ▶ Human resources
- ▶ Corporate communications
- ▶ Treasury/cash management
- ▶ Shareholder communications

These roles are recommended for a Priority 1 Data Compromise in which many parties may be involved, with individuals from within XYZ filling each defined role. For less significant Priority 2 events, these roles may be combined. The composition of the task force and its ability to accommodate all the various involved parties/responsibilities effectively will determine whether any of these roles should be consolidated or dismissed to ensure optimal efficiencies.

The other group that we have put together is the CIRP SWAT Team. Some organizations may call this their Computer Emergency Response Team (CERT). These are the various technical Subject Matter Experts (SMEs) that work in the different technologies that have a role with PCI data. The members of the CIRP SWAT team fall under the Technical Actions Coordinator. For the XYZ Corporation, several different technologies are involved with the input, storage, processing, and movement of PCI data. Each of these technologies needs representation on the CIRP SWAT team. This plan does not address the technical measures necessary to respond to the various alerts / events that may be an indicator of a breach.

Now that we've got the right people organized to do what is needed, we need to talk about a "battle rhythm," or more specifically, the OODA (observe, orient, decide, and act) loop. As mentioned in Chapter 1, a lot of folks need to get a lot of things done. They all can't waste their time sitting in on some conference call. There must be a prescribed time to talk about what's going on, make some decisions, and then turn people loose to get their jobs done.

Process and Rhythm

In the execution of this plan, participants should be able to anticipate what comes next. The following is the anticipated process for a Priority 1 data compromise:

Initiation phase (one-time)

▶ Initial incident notification

▶ Initial incident declaration

▶ Initial coordination conference call

▶ Formal assignment/allocation, commitment of resources: mobilization of the CIRP SWAT Team

Incident resolution phase (daily basis)

All times listed are P.M. unless noted and based on Pacific time.

▶ 9:00 A.M. – Informal update of significant events/actions from previous evening. Typically an e-mail to all.

▶ 11:00 A.M. – Coordinator synch-up. Typically a conference call with the three coordinators: incident, technical, and supporting.

▶ 2:00 – Decision brief conference call (as required) with any parties requiring a decision from the Incident Commander.

▶ 3:30 – Decision brief(s) inputs due to Incident Management Coordinator for inclusion in the 4:30 status/decision brief deck.

▶ 4:00 – Inputs for status report due from Supporting and Technical Coordinators to Incident Management Coordinator for inclusion into the 4:30 status/decision brief deck.

▶ 4:30 – Status report and (as required) decision brief(s) presented to Incident Commander.

▶ "Loop" as needed.

Incident termination phase (one-time)

▶ Decision to terminate incident

▶ Lessons learned submission(s)

▶ Incident metrics reporting

▶ Evidence retention

The preceding timeline includes that one-time event discussed in Chapter 5: you have detected indicators of a possible breach, analyzed events, and mobilized resources to respond. It also details a daily OODA loop in which the Incident Commander is briefed at 4:30. This is based on a once-a-day cycle. In the case of a malware outbreak, once a day probably isn't sufficient. It is up to you how often you want to conduct a meeting. You may do it twice a day initially and then once a day as things settle down. The idea here is you need to conduct your OODA loop so that management has the opportunity (and frequency) to manage, while the folks getting work done have sufficient time to take action.

The section that follows may or may not be of value to you. I have seen large military staffs run through status briefs of hundreds of PowerPoint slides. They cover a lot of material very quickly. I've also heard the argument (and agree with it to some detail) of "death by PowerPoint." I have a tendency to talk off topic, so I like PowerPoint presentations because they keep me on target. I've also had many CIRP call-outs (for Priority 2 incidents) that didn't need any formal presentation. So this is really up to you and how your organization works, and the severity of the incident you are responding to. If you find yourself in a situation such as that malware outbreak I described in Chapter 1, you may want to leverage the formality of PowerPoint slides to impose a structure that will hopefully create some discipline during your calls/meetings.

Following is a section of the CIRP that discusses both status and decision briefs. Specific examples of these briefs will be provided in the Appendix.

Synchronization and Decision-Making

Listed here are predefined templates for both decision and status briefs to be provided to the Incident Commander on a regular basis in the event of a malware outbreak.

Status Reports

The human cognitive process has been defined by some as the process of observation, orientation, decision, and action (OODA). For operational staffs, this process needs to repeat itself on a regular basis so that the task force is able to effectively evaluate and execute an actionable response to a crisis on an ongoing basis until the crisis is resolved. A key component of this OODA process is the status brief. The utilization of a cyclically scheduled status brief, which ensures sufficient time within the reporting cycle for the task force to execute assigned tasks, is the backbone of an operational response methodology.

All regular status updates given during the execution of the CIRP should use the dedicated Data Breach Status Brief PowerPoint slide deck. Each of the functional managers will update and present his/her respective slides during the status brief. This will ensure a more disciplined discussion and a more efficient exchange of information. These slides will also be posted to a shared location where all members of the task force and other interested parties can view a summary of the status.

The following rules apply when presenting during a status brief:

▶ Operational briefings are intended to be brief but comprehensive.

▶ The longer you take talking about what needs to be done, the less time you have to actually do it.

▶ Do not read your slides. Your slides should be self-explanatory.

▶ Highlight new information in red. Most of the presentation is repeated information.

▶ Be immediately available for questions when asked.

▶ Slides will be posted and available to everyone.

▶ A brief where all that you hear is "next slide please" is a GOOD brief.

▶ Submit your slides at least 15 minutes prior to the brief so the meeting organizer has time to prepare.

Decision Briefs

The objective of any operational response is to ensure the timely execution of actions. Often during high-tempo, high-stress operational events, a decision is needed that either cannot be reached through consensus within the task force or is of a serious enough impact that it should be made only by the Incident Commander. It is the role of the staff to prepare the Incident Commander to make this decision. The Data Breach Decision Brief PowerPoint deck should be used whenever a decision needs to be made by the Incident Commander.

The following guidelines should be followed whenever making a decision brief:

▶ The purpose of a decision brief is to empower the Incident Commander to make a decision.

▶ Provide a thorough discussion of the pros and cons (and appropriate timing) of required decisions.

▶ Examine *all* the options available, including not making a decision.

▶ Do not let personal bias limit your presentation. Your role is to provide the Incident Commander with sufficient information to make a decision, not to convince him/her of your inclination.

Here is an example of a decision brief format you could use:

> ## Decision Information
> - Decision-maker
> - Problem to be solved
> - Why we need to make this decision
> - Consequence of decision not being made
> - Decision coordinator

> ## Recommendation #1
> - Action to be taken
> - Known facts
> - Necessary assumptions
> - Pros/cons
> - Coordination required

> ## Recommendation #2
> - Action to be taken
> - Known facts
> - Necessary assumptions
> - Pros/cons
> - Coordination required

This type of structure may or may not be appropriate for your organization. Whether or not you choose to use PowerPoint slides does not relieve you of the requirement to perform status updates and to ensure that decisions are made. The fog of war and friction are the most prevalent challenges facing an organization in time of crisis. These are a couple of tools that you can use.

I've explained about ensuring that your plan is based on this idea of requirements-driven execution. In the case of a PCI data breach, you will be obligated at some time to notify parties outside of your organization. For example, you may need to notify your acquiring bank(s) of the breach. Organizations must be mindful of the various second- and third-order effects that come with meeting these notification obligations. The following section of the CIRP addresses both the required notifications but also the processes necessary to ensure the information you release will not adversely impact your organization.

The PCI template provided originally came from the VISA web site and it is dated, but I believe it is a very thorough format and I have kept it in my plan.

Mandatory Reporting/Notification(s)

Based on contractual and statutory obligations to which XYZ is subject, during a PCI compromise a number of reporting requirements may arise. These requirements are documented here. All PCI-related notifications should be routed through the Compliance group after having under gone the "Release of Public-Facing Documents" process detailed in the following.

Payment Card Industry Data Security Standard (PCI DSS)

In the event that XYZ has a data compromise or the suspected or confirmed loss or theft of any material records that contain cardholder data, the following notifications may be required of XYZ per Reference (7) Visa Notification Procedure:

1. Notify XYZ's acquiring bank immediately.
2. Notify Visa fraud investigations and incident management group immediately at (650) 123-4567.
3. Notify local office of United States Secret Service.
4. Provide an Incident Response Report document to XYZ's acquiring bank within three business days.
5. Provide all compromised Visa, Interlink, and Plus accounts to XYZ's acquiring bank within ten business days.
6. PCI Incident Report Template

I. Executive Summary

Include the following:

▶ Date of when forensic company was engaged

▶ Date(s) when forensic investigation began

▶ Location(s) visited or reviewed

▶ A brief summary of the environment reviewed. (Details should be documented under the Findings section.)

▶ If identified, list cause of intrusion

▶ Date(s) of intrusion

▶ List suspected cause of intrusion

▶ Specification as to whether or not the compromise has been contained

▶ Type of account information at risk

    ▶ Track 1 and Track 2

    ▶ PIN blocks

    ▶ CVV2

    ▶ Account number

    ▶ Expiration date

    ▶ Cardholder name

    ▶ Cardholder address

    ▶ Number of accounts at risk

    ▶ Timeframe of accounts at risk

(See a sample of Incident Dashboard on the following page.)

II. Background

▶ Brief summary of compromised entity company:

    ▶ Type of company

    ▶ Number of locations

    ▶ Parent company (if applicable)

III. PCI Status

Based on findings identified on the forensic investigation, indicate the compliance status for each of the 12 basic requirements under the CISP PCI Data Security Standard.

PCI Data Security Standard		
Requirements	**In Place**	**Not in Place**
Build and maintain a secure network		
Requirement 1: Install and maintain a firewall configuration to protect cardholder data		
Requirement 2: Do not use vendor-supplied defaults for system passwords and other security parameters		
Protect cardholder data		
Requirement 3: Protect stored cardholder data		
Requirement 4: Encrypt transmission of cardholder data across open, public networks		
Maintain a vulnerability management program		
Requirement 5: Use and regularly update anti-virus software		
Requirement 6: Develop and maintain secure systems and applications		
Implement strong access control measures		
Requirement 7: Restrict access to cardholder data by business need-to-know		
Requirement 8: Assign a unique ID to each person with computer access		
Requirement 9: Restrict physical access to cardholder data		
Regularly monitor and test networks		
Requirement 10: Track and monitor all access to network resources and cardholder data		
Requirement 11: Regularly test security systems and processes		
Maintain an information security policy		
Requirement 12: Maintain a policy that addresses information security		

IV Network Infrastructure overview

Provide a diagram of the network that includes the following:

► Cardholder data sent to central corporate server or data center

► Upstream connections to third-party processors

► Connections to Visa client bank networks

► Remote access connections by third-party vendors or internal staff

► Inbound/outbound network connectivity

► Network security controls and components (network security zones, firewalls, and so on)

► Clearly identify all infrastructure components implemented or modified after the timeframe of the compromise

V. Findings

► Provide specifics on firewall, infrastructure, host, and personnel findings.

► Identify any and all changes made to compromised entity's computing environment after the identification of a compromise.

    ► Provide specific dates of network, system, or Point of Sale (POS) changes.

    ► Include any and all forensic evidence supporting changes made to networks, systems, and POS components.

► Identify any data accessed by unauthorized parties.

► Identify any data exported by unauthorized parties.

► Identify any evidence of data deletion from systems involved in a compromise.

► If applicable, identify any deleted data recovered through forensic file recovery methods.

► Identify any third-party payment applications, including product version.

► Provide a timeline of incident events.

Release of "Public-Facing Documents"

Part of our response to a data compromise may be the release of public-facing documents. In a Priority 1 data compromise, this has the potential to cause significant notoriety that may damage the XYZ brand and its reputation in the marketplace. XYZ's legal and contractual obligations following such incidents may require the release of information that XYZ considers sensitive.

Examples of documents that may gain publicity include the following:

▶ PCI reports

▶ Statutory (such as CA SB-24, Federal HITECH) reports

▶ Notification to affected parties

▶ Responses to inquiries from third-party business partners (with network connections)

▶ Press releases

▶ Communication with law enforcement

▶ Communication with customers and shareholders

▶ Communication with employees

Draft/Approve/Release Process

When the obligation to release public-facing documents becomes known, a process should be in place to ensure that all releases of information from XYZ are thoughtfully created, verified for accuracy and relevancy, and formally approved by the corporation prior to its release. Every release of information must assume the worst case: that it will be on the front page of tomorrow's newspaper. To mitigate this risk, the process by which XYZ produces public-facing documents must be robust and thorough, no matter what the subject of the release.

The first step of this process is the drafting phase. Notice and disclosure documents must adhere to the legal and contractual requirements that arise from the incident. They must also be drafted in a manner that addresses the concerns of likely readers. Because many of the required PCI notifications require technical specifics, every effort must be made to ensure the technical accuracy of any publicly released document. Typically during the drafting phase legal, public affairs, and technical SMEs will be drawn upon to provide the content of the document.

Once a draft of the document is ready, it will become necessary for the document to be approved for accuracy, legal relevancy, and marketing/brand impact. There is never a perfect document. During the approval process, the various authorities should work to reach compromises on the actual document. The end result of the approval process is that key technical, legal, and Public affairs SMEs approve of the document prior to its release to the public.

An important consideration prior to the release of any information is the potential operational and brand implications. It may be best to notify the organization in advance of the release. As a result of both the T.J.Maxx and Hannaford compromises, advertisements were released to assure customers. It is incumbent upon the Incident Commander to ensure that prior to the release of any information to the public, efforts have been made to inform and prepare other potentially affected entities both within and outside of the organization.

Once all the necessary SMEs have crafted and approved the public-facing document, and the Incident Commander has ensured that all efforts have been made to anticipate any impact on the corporation from such a release, the document should be forwarded via legal, to public affairs for public dissemination. In the circumstances of PCI notifications, compliance will work with public affairs to ensure the document reaches the specific PCI entities (that is, acquiring banks.) Any document that leaves XYZ with potential for public dissemination must be routed via legal to public affairs prior to leaving XYZ regardless of its purpose or content.

Public-Facing Documents Participants

Creation and Approval—Suggested participants:

► Public affairs

► Legal

► Compliance

► Technical SMEs

► Advertising

► Investor relations

Release authority: Public affairs

Recommended notification prior to release:

► Investor relations

► Retail operations

► Internal communications

► Customer service center

► Government affairs

► Consumer insights

Another serious consideration you should undertake as a CIRP response cell is the decision to notify senior management. The prevailing thought you should have is that you don't want your CEO first hearing about your breach on the front page of the local newspaper. As discussed in the beginning of this book, preparation can help smart executives recognize that bad news can be good news in disguise—when it can be used constructively to help protect the organization. Depending on the size of your organization and the nature of the incident, you may or may not choose to notify senior management formally. I have almost quarterly incidents involving the loss of sensitive information. Each has the potential to hit the media, but in many cases, we don't formally notify senior management. Typically, the scope of data lost is small and the likelihood of negative press is minimal. This is one of those decisions the CIRP team will need to make.

The task of formally notifying senior management should not be taken lightly. If you are in a small organization, this may be less relevant to you. If you work in a large organization, this is not a trivial task. I exercise this activity regularly as part of our annual PCI CIRP test. This is a very interesting effort. Depending on the size of your organization, you probably can't simply walk into your CEO's office and tell him/her you have a problem. For very large organizations, the CEO may not even be directly informed. During our latest CIRP test, we determined that three people would be formally informed: the chief audit officer, the chief legal (who is also chief privacy) officer, and the chief finance officer. This all depends on your organization and is something you should investigate and test.

Another byproduct of testing the notification of senior management was the development of what we call the "Management Checklist." During one of our annual tests of the CIRP, the CISO at the time was concerned that prior to notifying senior management we should ensure that we had all of our technical ducks in a row—the concern being that once we brought this topic to senior management, we had to be sure we had confirmed that all the various PCI technologies were checked to ensure that they were either involved in the breach or outside of the scope. We developed a technology agnostic checklist for this purpose, and every member of the CIRP SWAT team is tested to ensure they have the necessary procedures to answer the questions. The "Management Checklist" is listed as Tab J and a copy is in the Appendix of this book.

The following is listed in our CIRP:

At some point, members of the CIRP Response Team will need to formally notify senior management that the organization has been breached and significant data has been lost. This notification has significant implications, both for the senior leadership of the corporation and the senior leadership of the CIRP Response Team. This formal notification should be made only with the approval of the Incident Commander and formally submitted to senior leadership via the reviewing senior executive.

The Management Checklist (Tab J) was developed for this requirement. The purpose of the checklist is to ensure that all platforms/technologies that have PCI data or may be involved in the breach have had an initial examination that would sufficiently identify the scope of the breach. This checklist is technology agnostic and is not meant to be all inclusive and should not be construed as a full investigation.

All PCI systems should be evaluated against the Management Checklist/Tab J prior to notification of senior mgmt.

One of the key objectives of any CIRP is to prepare the organization for post-event legal implications. These can include both criminal prosecution and civil litigation. Your plan should include thorough evidence procedures. This CIRP does not go into detail about the evidence procedures for the organization. That is a separate topic and can be subject of a book in and of itself. The plan does refer to the XYZ Corporation's internal forensics and evidence procedures.

Evidence Discovery and Retention

Criminal Prosecution

XYZ's Legal Division and Loss Prevention Departments will determine the manner and identify the assets required to assist and cooperate in the efforts of responsible law enforcement agencies investigating an incident. Typically, the lead law enforcement agency will want to create and take forensic copies—or, if possible, the actual physical item—of all affected technical components into custody. Law enforcement efforts may extend into the physical workspace of suspected employees.

More details are provided in the sections below under "Liaison with Local Law Enforcement" and "Evidence Gathering and Handling."

Civil Litigation

The potential for post-event litigation is a serious concern for any corporation. All information regarding the status of the enterprise at the time of the compromise and the organization's response to the data compromise is potential evidence.

It is the responsibility of XYZ corporate legal counsel to provide recommendations to the members of the CIRP response team regarding the treatment of all information accumulated during the response to the data compromise. No item pertaining to the data compromise or XYZ's response should be deleted or destroyed without the consent of the Legal Division. If an item must be deleted from a system to preserve security or data integrity, a copy of that item should be preserved in a forensically sound manner whenever possible.

Managing Evidence

Everything done in response to the data compromise is potentially evidence. Task force members should make every effort to document their actions. Persons and departments involved in the data compromise response will create a unique folder for all incident response related e-mails and files. All hard copy records will also be stored separately for future collection. Files, e-mails and other documents pertaining to the data compromise should not be deleted or otherwise destroyed unless approved by XYZ legal counsel. All parties examining logs or any item that may contain specific information regarding the compromise should be familiar with References 7 and 8 and the section titled "Evidence Gathering and Handling."

Within the execution of this plan, XYZ has two resources that will provide critical assistance and guidance with regards to evidence. XYZ Corporate Loss Prevention has the responsibility to be the CIRP Evidence SME. Because they routinely work with law enforcement and most of their members have previous law enforcement experience, one of their primary tasks will be to ensure that the CIRP task force follows proper evidence procedures.

XYZ also has a Forensic SME within InfoSec. The Forensic SME is XYZ's expert at extracting evidence from computer systems. As part of this field of expertise, the Forensics SME has expert evidence-handling knowledge and is the author of References 8 and 9. The InfoSec Forensic SME will also be relied upon to ensure proper evidence handling procedures are followed by the CIRP Task Force.

Another decision you will need to make during a cyber-crisis is the decision to reach out to law enforcement. The next section is from the actual CIRP:

Liaison with Local Law Enforcement

Understanding the role of law enforcement (LE) during a data compromise can be difficult. Issues such as jurisdiction, technical competency, and availability of resources are all factors when working with law enforcement.

The first step in a criminal event is filing a police report. Typically, based on where the crime occurred, the local law enforcement agency would have physical jurisdiction and take an initial police report. However, jurisdiction has the potential to be a difficult distinction. If, for example, a perpetrator gains access to the XYZ wireless network in Colorado, to compromise a print server in Seattle, to eventually download credit card numbers off a system in Phoenix, the determination of physical jurisdiction can be subject to debate and "passing the buck" within LE.

Once a crime has been reported, statutory jurisdictions are taken into consideration in addition to the physical jurisdiction. Since a data compromise may be in violation of federal law, agencies such as the FBI or Secret Service may also have a role to play in any criminal investigation.

The third consideration is technical resources. Due to the complex nature of computer crimes, few local law enforcement agencies have the staff to address high tech crimes adequately. Many local agencies fall under the support of regional computer crime task forces. In the Northern California region, for example, the Northern California Computer Crimes Task Force (NC3TF) is such a resource. At the federal level, the Secret Service and FBI have the technical resources and national (and international) capabilities.

However, obtaining the support of either a regional or federal law enforcement resource should not be taken for granted. The local agency is obligated to take a report (assuming you find one that assumes jurisdiction). Regional, state, and federal law enforcement resources may have minimum criteria for committing resources to a criminal investigation. One criteria for law enforcement in any effort to investigate and eventually prosecute a criminal act(s) is the victim's willingness to cooperate.

XYZ Loss Prevention (LE Liaison)

The company's primary contact with law enforcement will be dependent on the type and scale of the incident. Most contact will be handled by the local division Loss Prevention Department, who will work closely with the Corporate Loss Prevention Department. In the case of a Priority 1 event, the initial primary contact for law enforcement will be the Corporate Loss Prevention Department. For the execution of this plan, all LE liaisons will work through Corporate Loss Prevention.

Law Enforcement Points of Contact (POC) (Tab I)

Under no circumstances should anyone but Loss Prevention attempt to contact the following:

Rapid Enforcement Allied Computer Team Task Force (REACT) – South Bay

POC: John Johnson (408) 555-1234 or Sgt. Mike Michaels (408) 123-4567

Northern California Computer Crimes Task Force (NC3TF) – Carly Carlton (707) 123-6789 or EMAIL@nc.org

US Secret Service
San Francisco Field Office
Special Agent Molly Malloy
Electronic Crimes Task Force
(415) 555-1234
EMAIL@information.usss.gov

US Secret Service
San Francisco Field Office
Special Agent Jason James
(415) 555-2345/(415) 123-4567
EMAIL@USSS.DHS.gov

FBI Oakland Division
Computer Crimes
POC: Barry Barrett
(510) 123-6789
EMAIL@ic.fbi.gov

FBI Phoenix Division
Computer Crimes
POC: Keri Kimble
(602) 555-1234

You should also refer back to the discussion in Chapter 3 about reaching out to your local law enforcement resources before you have a crisis.

The next section of the CIRP discusses those technical actions required for the containment, eradication, and recovery of affected IT systems. The following information is not meant to be deeply technical. It is, however, intended to give everyone on the CIRP response team an idea of how each of their roles relates to others' roles. A wealth of information surrounds the technical aspects of Incident Response.

In developing this part of the CIRP, I leveraged the NIST (National Institute of Standards and Technology) manual on computer incident response (Special Publication 800-61). As mentioned previously in the chapter, all technical efforts must be mindful of their possible impact on evidence.

Listed next are the sections of the CIRP.

Incident Containment, Eradication, and Recovery

The XYZ (Data Compromise) CIRP SWAT Team

Key technical SMEs from all the PCI-scoped applications have been identified and trained to support the technical execution of the CIRP. Their initial task is to perform a technology agnostic "Management Checklist" (Tab J) to verify the security of their respective systems. This information is referenced in the report to senior management. Members of the CIRP SWAT team should remain engaged as the core technical SMEs during the execution of this CIRP.

Containment

XYZ shall identify containment strategies to control an incident's impact to compromised systems, limit the extent of the incident, prevent further damage, and regain normal operations of affected systems. Containment measures shall also be evaluated against the potential loss or corruption of security incident evidence. Containment methods include the following:

▶ Ensuring redundant systems and data have not been compromised

▶ Monitoring system and network activity

▶ Disabling access to compromised shared file systems

- ► Disabling specific system services
- ► Changing passwords or disabling accounts
- ► Temporarily shutting down the compromised or at risk system
- ► Disconnecting compromised or at risk systems from the network

Identification and Isolation of Affected System(s)

The first step in any containment strategy is to identify systems that have been affected by a cyber-attack. What host(s) has been compromised? What network(s) is involved? How far did the attackers get? What level of privileges did they attain? Understanding the root cause of the compromise(s) is the bridge to the process of eradication and recovery. Not all compromises are the result of a "hacker" exploiting a vulnerability from within a system. Some data compromises are the result of a trusted insider using their authority improperly.

Verification of Nonaffected Systems

Once it is determined which system(s) was compromised and the root cause of the compromise, a secondary responsibility for the data compromise task force is to verify that other PCI and adjacent systems have not also been compromised. Often attackers will "leap frog" from various systems to get to the desired data. Remediation of the primary affected system without investigating other potentially compromised systems may leave the corporation susceptible to repeat attacks.

Intruders regularly establish more entry points into a network once they have gained initial access. Whenever an attack or an intrusion is detected, all other systems that are similar to the system that was accessed should be checked. "Similar" can have various meanings depending on your operational environment, including the following:

- ► Systems that are in the same IP address range or are on the same network segment. Intruders perform scans across large ranges of IP addresses to locate security vulnerabilities.

- ► Systems that are in the same "trusted" domain. These systems provide access to users from other systems within the same domain without further authentication.

- ► Systems that have at least one network service in common. Intruders often check for well-known services such as DNS (Domain Name System), FTP (File Transfer Protocol), HTTP (Hyper-Text Transfer Protocol), and SMTP (Simple Mail Transfer Protocol).

- ► Systems that have the same operating system.

Third-Party and External Connections

As the task force endeavors to determine the root cause and access method of the data compromise, attention should be paid to third-party networks and extranets as possible entry points for the intrusion or a possible vector of additional infection or movement to those systems.

Third-party connections are listed within the Tab D Third-Party Connections.

Appropriate notification should be provided to parties listed in Tab D who manage third-party connections. The task force should anticipate questions coming from those entities that are connected to the network being apprehensive about the spread of whatever means or technology that was responsible for the compromise transferring into their environment. Depending on the NDA (nondiscloure agreement) status of these third parties, the CIRP team may consider following the "release of public-facing information" process prior to notifying external partners without existing NDAs.

Once you have determined the scope of your compromise, your next step is eradication and recovery so that your system(s) can be returned to a noncompromised state.

Eradication and Recovery

Remediation

Incidents that are classified as High Priority Incidents are communicated to the ICC and to Operations for further action.

High-priority incidents are assigned to separate teams which consist of second- and third-level support staff, members of the CIRP SWAT team, as well as Data Center Ops, Business Relationship Managers (BRMs), and Field Services.

Compensating Controls

In the event of a data compromise, XYZ may need to implement compensating controls consisting of either a device or combination of devices, applications, processes, and controls that meet basic operational requirements:

1. Provide additional segmentation/abstraction (for example, at the network layer).

2. Provide ability to restrict access to cardholder data or databases based on the following criteria:

   ▶ IP address/MAC address

   ▶ Application/service

   ▶ User accounts/groups

   ▶ Data type (packet filtering)

3. Restrict logical access to the database.

   ▶ Control logical access to the database independent of Active Directory or Lightweight Directory Access Protocol (LDAP)

4. Additional logging/monitoring on all logs including system, application, and database.

5. Increased monitoring of security infrastructure logs such as firewall and IDS/IPS alerts.

Another area that is a critical consideration when you are responding to a breach is the avoidance of unintended consequences on the operating environment that may impact the key functions of the organization. In short, make sure that your cure isn't worse than the disease. There are many reasons to include your Disaster Recovery group into your CIRP response effort. For one, if you have to take a system off-line for either evidence or restoral purposes, you should include the appropriate DR capability to minimize impact to the organization. The other reason is as you come to make decisions regarding technical actions, you must have an understanding of the consequences of your actions on the business. Most DR groups maintain detailed business impact analyses of the various systems in the organization. It's imperative that you remain vigilant of the impact your actions may have on the organization's "center of gravity." Listed next is the section of the CIRP referencing Disaster Recovery.

Disaster Recovery/Business Continuity

Sometimes the most efficient mechanism to recover from a compromised system is to cut over to a backup system. This enables the business processes to resume while allowing the data compromise investigation to continue. In circumstances where Law Enforcement subpoenas identify devices as evidence, this may prove to be the only option for a timely restoration of service. Prior to cutting over to the backup system, you must ensure that the replacement system does not have the same exploitation and/or vulnerability used to compromise the original system, because that would enable the new (backup) system to be attacked. If you are unable to verify the absence of the exploit/vulnerability, additional compensating controls are warranted.

A summary of each PCI systems Disaster Recovery capability and POCs is listed in Tab (K) *Disaster Recovery Summary*.

The last section I want to discuss came as the result of an auditor's finding. Per the PCI DSS, the auditor interpreted a requirement that the roles and responsibilities for all participants should be listed out as part of the plan. We complied with the auditor's request and here is what we listed in the plan.

CIRP Roles and Responsibilities

The following Roles and Responsibilities are developed specifically for the execution of the CIRP during a Priority 1 data compromise. During a Priority 2 compromise, additional considerations will be provided as to the scope and relevance of all the actions listed here. During a Priority 2 compromise, a more scaled-down effort should be anticipated.

Advertising

While working for the Supporting Actions Coordinator...

► In an effort to reduce the impact of a Priority 1 data compromise on the XYZ brand...

   ► Monitor and provide advice during the "release of public-facing documentation" actions of the CIRP.

   ► Be prepared to develop and launch marketing efforts to counter adverse brand impact of data compromise event.

Compliance

▶ Perform the role of Supporting Actions Coordinator in accordance with IAW, the CIRP must do the following:

  ▶ Ensure that all statutory and contractual obligations are met in a timely manner.

  ▶ Provide a single POC to the incident commander for all CIRP supporting actions IAW the CIRP.

  ▶ Work with Finance/Cash Management as the single POC for the acquiring banks and providing the appropriate PCI documentation.

Corporate Accounting

While working for the Supporting Actions Coordinator...

▶ Ensure that all SOX requirements are met.

Disaster Recovery

While working for the Technical Actions Coordinator"...

▶ Maintain situational awareness throughout the entire CIRP execution of the Disaster Recovery/Business Continuity (DR/BC) status of affected PCI technologies.

▶ Provide proactive "consequence management" and coordination with affected PCI technology groups to ensure they are capable of rapid transition to DR/BC mode.

▶ Coordinate with Loss Prevention to ensure they have a current assessment of each affected technology's ability to support the seizure of physical assets by Law Enforcement.

Human Resources

While working for the Supporting Actions Coordinator...

▶ In the event that the scope of the CIRP response involves punitive and/or LE actions against a XYZ employee...

  ▶ Provide guidance regarding the appropriate actions in dealing with such an employee(s).

Incident Control Center (ICC)

▶ Perform the role of Technical Actions Coordinator IAW the CIRP...

  ▶ Identify, contact, and coordinate XYZ technical SMEs in support of (ISO) the CIRP response.

  ▶ Serve as the single POC to the Incident Commander for all technical actions.

Information Security Forensics

While working for the Supporting Actions Coordinator...

▶ Oversee all Forensics requirements ISO (In Support Of) the CIRP.

▶ Coordinate the forensic efforts of any third-party resources ISO the CIRP.

▶ Working with Loss Prevention, provide expert guidance relative to evidence procedures when appropriate.

▶ Collect evidence from involved parties upon termination of CIRP response.

▶ Ensure the following supporting documents are current:

   ▶ Reference (8) XYZ Digital Evidence Verification

   ▶ Reference (9) XYZ Digital Evidence Chain of Custody Procedure

Information Security Operations Center (ISOC)

▶ Manage the day-to-day monitoring of critical systems for potential security compromises.

▶ Serve as central POC for suspected security compromises:

   ▶ Conduct analysis of suspected data compromises IAW this plan.

   ▶ Perform Incident Declaration and Documentation functions as defined in this plan.

▶ ISOC Manager: Perform the role of the Incident Management Coordinator during a data compromise.

Internal Communications

While working for the Supporting Actions Coordinator, in an effort to reduce the impact of a data compromise on the XYZ operations...

▶ Monitor and provide advice during the "release of public-facing documentation" actions of the CIRP.

▶ Be prepared to develop and release internal communications within XYZ to prepare customer-facing employees to counter potentially adverse impact of data compromise event.

Investor Relations

While working for the Supporting Actions Coordinator...

▶ Provide guidance during the "release of public-facing documents" process.

▶ Ensure that all Shareholder messaging requirements are met.

▶ Ensure all SEC reporting requirements are addressed by the CIRP team.

IT

In support of the Technical Actions Coordinator...

▶ Provide the necessary technical SME support to enable an effective response to a Data Compromise

  ▶ Affected PCI applications

  ▶ Affected platforms

  ▶ NOC and networking support

  ▶ Database support

  ▶ Network security engineering support

  ▶ Other IT support necessary to resolve the data compromise

IT Retail Portfolio

In support of the Technical Actions Coordinator...

▶ Provide ongoing liaison with affected XYZ business groups as to CIRP efforts and progress.

▶ Provide necessary input regarding potential business impact of CIRP response.

▶ Working with DR, coordinate between IT and affected business unit(s) in the event of a disruption to the business operations that may require a DR/BC action.

Legal

While working for the Supporting Actions Coordinator...

▶ Provide ongoing legal counsel to the CIRP task force:

  ▶ Provide specific guidance ensuring that current actions are supportive of possible post-event litigation.

  ▶ Provide specific guidance ensuring that current actions are supportive of possible post-event criminal prosecution.

▶ Provide specific guidance with regard to involving LE in the CIRP response.

▶ Provide guidance as to XYZ's current statutory and contractual obligations.

▶ Assist in the determination to involve Law Enforcement.

▶ Act as the repository of all incident-related evidence upon termination of the response.

Loss Prevention

As part of your day-to-day activities:

▶ Notify InfoSec of any suspected data compromises.

▶ Inform InfoSec of all non-actionable/informal events that involve sensitive data.

While working for the Supporting Actions Coordinator...

▶ Perform the function of Law Enforcement liaison IAW the CIRP.

▶ Work with HR in the event of punitive/LE actions against XYZ employee(s).

▶ Working with Information Security Forensics, assist the role of Evidence SME during the execution of the CIRP.

Problem Management

▶ Support the Incident Management Coordinator by providing an analysis of the CIRP execution to identify improvements (Lessons Learned) for the CIRP.

▶ Assist in the definition and measurement of performance metrics during the execution of the CIRP.

▶ Conduct problem analysis of failure in InfoSec infrastructure that may have enabled the data compromise to occur.

Public Affairs

While working for the Supporting Actions Coordinator in an effort to reduce the impact of a P1 data compromise on the XYZ brand...

▶ Monitor and provide advice during the "release of public-facing documentation" actions of the CIRP.

▶ Be prepared to develop and release notifications to counter adverse customer impact of event.

▶ Serve as the POC for all media queries.

Retail Operations

While working for the "Supporting Actions Coordinator" in an effort to reduce the impact of a P1 data compromise on the XYZ retail operations...

- ▶ Monitor and provide operational impact input during the execution of the CIRP.
- ▶ In conjunction with the IT Retail Portfolio BRMs, provide ongoing liaison to retail operations management at all levels as to the status and implications of the ongoing CIRP response.

Reviewing Senior Executive

Having been designated by the incident commander...

- ▶ Provide detached oversight of CIRP efforts and results.
- ▶ Influence the current response effort where shortcomings are apparent (that is, by directing additional resources, and so on).
- ▶ Assist the Incident Commander with providing on going liaison to senior IT and business leadership within XYZ Inc.
- ▶ Identify and take corrective action if current staffing/effort is insufficient/ineffective.

XYZ CISO

- ▶ Senior Executive with overall responsibility for the preparation, maintenance, and execution of this plan.
- ▶ Perform the role of Incident Commander during a data compromise IAW the CIRP.
- ▶ Facilitate the establishment of a Reviewing Senior Executive IAW the CIRP.
- ▶ Chair the daily status brief.
- ▶ As required, chair and provide timely direction during decision briefs.
- ▶ Maintain ongoing liaison with senior IT and business management as to progress of CIRP response.
- ▶ Approve the release of all public-facing documents.
- ▶ Decide to engage law enforcement.
- ▶ Terminate the CIRP response.

This wraps up the chapter on executing the data breach CIRP. Again, this is not meant to be the "answer," but hopefully this will give you an idea of how a CIRP can be written to fit particular circumstances and will give you some idea of what you should come up with to support your organization in time of crisis. The next chapter will cover those actions you need to keep your plan current and tested.

Your Data Breach CIRP: Post Incident Planning and Maintenance

W̲e are finally at the last section of the Data Breach CIRP. We have spoken previously about preparing for crisis and the execution of the CIRP during time of actual crisis. This section of the plan covers four main areas:

▶ Determining when an incident is really over

▶ Maintaining the currency of your plan

▶ Learning from executing and testing your plan ("Lessons Learned")

▶ Testing your plan

Ultimately, your crisis will come to pass. It's a good idea to document what criteria needs to be met in order for an incident to be terminated. This helps you in a couple of ways: As you progress through your incident, you have an idea of the criteria that will be used to terminate the incident. If you are the incident coordinator, this is something you should start tracking as you see things winding down. The second reason is that often after an incident, folks are basically in a hurry to wrap things up and move on. This is another point of friction. You risk losing resources toward the end of your incident because folks may think things are done and they have day jobs to go back to. Having a pre-agreed definition of success helps you hold the response together until your crisis is truly resolved. This is something you put together with your advisory committee when you build your plan. Listed next is what I have in the CIRP.

Post-Incident Activity

Incident Termination

Prior to terminating a data compromise response, it is critical to ensure that all due diligence has been performed. The termination phase of a data compromise is a critical time to ensure that all the necessary actions have been performed, that all requirements for evidence retention have been identified, and that all applicable standards have been met in resolving the computer data compromise.

Criteria for Terminating an Incident

The criteria for terminating an incident are as follows:

▶ Was the source of the compromise identified, contained, and eradicated?

▶ Did we confirm that other XYZ systems were not affected?

▶ Have all the required notifications occurred?

▶ Are there any significant activities outstanding that require the immediate attention of the Data Compromise Task Force to resolve?

▶ What systems and/or processes failed to prevent, detect, and/or correct the compromise of the affected system?

▶ Have the appropriate changes been made to prevent future occurrences of the compromise from affecting XYZ systems?

▶ Has a discussion with members of the data compromise task force occurred, and was there consensus that the data compromise incident has been resolved?

Decision Process for Terminating an Incident

The formal process for terminating an incident is as follows: It is based on the incident termination criteria listed above, uses the decision brief process as defined in "Synchronization and Decision-Making" section, and includes the following members of the task force (or their successors):

Function	POC	Minor Mobilization	Major Mobilization
CISO	Charles Jones	Involved	Involved
Mgr ISOC	Armando Jones	Involved	Involved
Legal	Ray Jones	Involved	Involved
Compliance	Elwin Jones	Informed	Involved
Loss Prevention	John Jones	Informed	Involved
Public Affairs	Brad Jones	Informed	Involved
IT Retail Portfolio	Diana Jones	Informed	Informed
Investor relations	Mary Jones	As Required	Informed
Disaster Recovery	Ian Jones	As Required	As Required
Corp Acctg (SOX)	Dennis Jones	As Required	As Required
Advertising	Kim Jones	As Required	As Required
HR	Michele Jones	As Required	As Required
Cash Management	Dennis Jones	As Required	As Required

"Involved" members are required to provide input regarding the termination of the incident to the incident commander. "As required" members may be requested to participate in the incident termination process. Informed members are copied on all actions involving the termination and have the discretion to involve themselves in the decision to terminate the plan due to SME concerns they may have.

The Incident Commander will ultimately make the decision to terminate the incident based on the recommendations presented to him/her by the members of the Task Force listed above.

This last section of the CIRP is the smallest but seems to take the largest amount of individual and organizational commitment. The constant maintaining and improving of a plan is one of the more difficult tasks to accomplish. All too often, plans are written and placed on a shelf, only to be forgotten. The compliance box is checked and the InfoSec person moves on to other tasks. Over time, as the organization changes and requirements change, the plan becomes outdated only to be irrelevant when it is needed later. One of the most important concepts that needs to be conveyed is that your plan is a living document and requires frequent attention. We're going to discuss this topic in greater detail, but first here is what is recorded in the actual CIRP:

Plan Maintenance

Overview

This plan is valuable only as long as it is relevant. The objective of maintaining a plan is to ensure that at time of immediate execution, the plan provides relevant information to ensure successful execution. To this end, it is incumbent upon all those who will be potentially called to respond to a data compromise to ensure that plan information for which they are responsible is current and relevant.

Regular Updates

Verification/Updates of Perishable Data

The ISOC is responsible for verifying the currency of all components of this plan to ensure the information necessary for the execution of this plan is always current. Upgrade information will be listed in the "Updating and Synchronization" table in the "Plan Structure" section listed previously in the "Plan Introduction" portion of the plan.

Incorporation of Previous Lessons Learned

Lessons Learned input should be tracked by the ISOC for inclusion into subsequent versions of the computer incident response plan.

Prior to including any recommendation made in a Lessons Learned, it is imperative that the recommendation be socialized to all participants of the plan for their approval.

Lesson Learned recommendations should be e-mailed to the primary participants (those defined as "involved" in the Priority 1 Mobilization matrix) for their input. The CISO has final approval authority for implementing a Lessons Learned recommendation. The manager of the ISOC is responsible for acceptance, tracking, routing, coordinating the decision-making process, and including successful recommendations into the updated version of the data compromise incident response plan.

Annual Testing of the Plan

Requirement

PCI DSS v1.2 and industry best practices require that all incident response plans be tested on an annual basis. Plan validation typically requires the involvement of all anticipated participants to ensure that if the plan were to be executed, it would have current information, work within the current structure and staffing of XYZ, and would be immediately executable as written.

Exercise Mechanics

An incident response plan can be exercised in a number of ways. The U.S. military spends millions of dollars testing contingency plans for potential crises around the globe. These very complex exercises involve persons who would be expected to execute the plan, simulated potential adversaries, control persons simulating external entities that would influence the execution of the plan, and evaluators of the performance of personnel executing the plan. These large-scale exercises evaluate both the plan and the persons anticipated to execute the plan.

The objective within XYZ is to evaluate the plan and not the participants. The annual test should focus on the following objectives:

▶ Is the information in the plan current and relevant?

▶ Are the processes listed within the plan effective within the current XYZ environment?

▶ Are the proper persons involved in the execution of the plan?

▶ Are the processes listed in the plan current with the industry standard/best practices?

▶ Have we exposed the plan to all potentially involved parties from within XYZ and outside partners/participants for their validation?

Lessons Learned

At a minimum, during the annual testing of the plan, the ISOC needs to present a summary of all Lessons Learned from the previous year and the status of each. This serves as a mechanism to validate for the submitter, members of the task force, and the CISO that all Lessons Learned for the previous year have been accounted for and that the Lessons Learned effort is taken seriously by XYZ.

During the annual testing of the data compromise incident response plan, Lessons Learned input should be collected and processed according to the procedure listed above.

Record(s) Retention

All records pertaining to the maintenance of the incident response plan should be retained by XYZ. In the event it becomes necessary to demonstrate XYZ's commitment to performing the necessary due diligence, information regarding all Lessons Learned inputs, and annual test documentation shall be maintained by the ISOC and available for inspection.

The preceding section is listed in the actual plan. Let me take the opportunity to provide more insight to this topic. One of the first actions mentioned is "Verification and Updates to perishable data." Chapter 5 discussed this topic briefly. The following table includes information that can serve as an important tool in maintaining your plan. Listed here are the various sources of information your plan calls upon to be relevant.

Document	Last Verification	Responsible Party
Ref (1) NIST Guide	2/25/11	ISOC
Ref (2) DHS NIPP	2/25/11	ISOC
Ref (3) DOJ Handbook	2/25/11	ISOC
Ref (4) XYZ Crisis Communications SOP	3/23/12	Corp Public Affairs
Ref (5) CSO Magazine Article on Data Compromise Notification Letters	N/A	N/A
Ref (6) XYZ Malware Mitigation SOP	5/19/11	ISOC
Ref (7) VISA Procedure	2/25/11	Compliance
Ref (8) XYZ Digital Evidence Verification	5/30/11	XYZ Forensics
Ref (9) XYZ Digit Evidence Chain of Custody Procedure	5/30/11	XYZ Forensics
Ref (10) Third-party Security PFI Services SOW	5/19/11	ISOC
Encl (1) PCI Data flow	5/30/11	Compliance
Encl (2) Web posting by Hannaford CEO	N/A	N/A
Encl (3) XYZ Mutual Nondisclosure Agreement	3/23/12	VMO
Tab (A) Compliance and Statutory Framework Document	5/30/8	Compliance
Tab (B) ISOC Threat Portfolio	3/22/11	ISOC
Tab (C) PCI Log Data Retention	1/1/12	ISOC
Tab (D) Third Party Connections	11/4/11	ISOC
Tab (E) Sample Data Compromise Notification letters	N/A	ISOC
Tab (F) ISOC Monitoring Feeds Summary	5/30/11	ISOC
Tab (G) Incident Notification POCs	5/19/11	ISOC
Tab (H) Key Resource Escalation/Back-up Instruction	5/30/11	ISOC
Tab (I) Law Enforcement Points of Contact (POC)	5/19/11	Loss Prevention
Tab (J) CIRP SWAT Management Checklist	1/14/12	ISOC
Tab (K) Disaster Recovery Summary	3/22/011	ISOC

Every quarter I try to go through this list. Some items don't require constant upgrading, but most do. It is imperative that you keep this list accurate. At a minimum, during time of crisis, you will know by looking at this how *out of date* you are and it may provide you ideas of where you need to focus your efforts in *catching up*.

The second area I want to discuss is *Lessons Learned*. This is how you keep your plan relevant over time. As the organization changes, people change. Some of your key roles within your plan will see the assigned person change. They bring with them different ideas of how things should be done. Lessons Learned, whether from testing the plan or actually executing the plan, is the mechanism by which the plan *lives and grows*. I use the Marine Corps format of Topic, Discussion, and Recommendation. You start out with a one- or two-sentence topic that is basically the 5 W's (who, what, …) you want to address. The next section is discussion, which allows you to put the topic into some sort of context so that everyone can understand what it is you are trying to suggest. The third and final section is the recommendation. This is where you actually document what should change. It is not enough to say there is a problem; you need to recommend a solution. This shouldn't be more than a couple of pages. Typically, I will solicit ideas from participants of either an incident or a test. I will then put them into this format and e-mail it out to all of the participants of the plan. If there are no objections, I incorporate them into the next version of the CIRP. If there is some contention, then usually I will incorporate the suggestion into the next test of the plan. This way, all participants can focus on the topic.

This is a good segue into the next topic of the regular testing of your plan. Someone could write a book on testing. I have been a participant when the military tested its plans. They call them *exercises* and they involve thousands of people and are extremely detailed. They have full-time staffs that are dedicated to nothing but setting up and executing these tests. Their goal is the same as yours: to test the relevancy of the anticipation, collaboration, and research previously performed to prepare for a crisis. In the CIRP content above, you can see that I believe in scenario-based testing. This is not the only way to do it. There really isn't a defined standard for testing a plan. If you are an organization that falls under the Payment Card Industry (PCI), your PCI auditor may have an idea of what they want, but that is different from auditor to auditor.

So let's talk about an annual data breach CIRP test. The first thing you will need is plenty of notice if you are going to get everyone on your team in one place at one time.

Here's how I do it: I usually book 10:00 to 2:00 and provide lunch and plenty of breaks so folks can attend to their primary day jobs. Once I get a date that works, I'll send out a "save the date" e-mail 4–6 weeks in advance. I will follow up a week or so out with a PowerPoint regarding the exercise. Typically, everyone knows that this is a PCI requirement so I don't get much push back. You may want to consider a "why we need to do this" slide at the top of your PowerPoint deck. I usually like to list objectives on a slide. Over 12 months of time, you typically need to address many issues.

This last annual exercise I needed to address the following objectives:

► At a minimum, I needed to confirm that everyone I had listed in the plan was still around and hadn't left the company or their job hadn't changed.

► Two folks were new to the plan (they assumed new roles) and I needed to make sure they had a chance to focus on the plan and walk through it.

► We needed to work through a couple of Lessons Learned from previous incidents (Priority 2).

► I wanted to focus more on the notification of Senior Management.

My next slide detailed the scenario and timeline. I took a scenario from the newspaper. An insider at Bank of America stole and sold a bunch of customer data. I like it when I can point to something that happened to someone else, because I've seen a lot of time wasted when folks start to question/doubt the scenario. The scenario is a tool that helps folks work through the plan. It provides a context for them. Folks get too worked up when the scenario isn't ideal.

I also like to include a slide with assumptions and limitations regarding the test. This is just a simple test. There's plenty of "what about this?" issues you should deal with up front by putting them on this slide. I usually review previous Lessons Learned so the collective has an idea of what's been learned previously.

At the end of the exercise, I provide the PCI auditor a copy of the slides, a list of attendees, and any new lessons learned from the test as evidence of the annual test.

I would like to add a couple of additional comments on conducting a test of your CIRP. I wish I could give you a simple format to use, but I can't. I've been doing annual tests for the past several years. Some go according to plan and others are like herding cats. The goal is to get people thinking and talking about the plan. Everyone in the room has valuable information to contribute. Don't panic if things get off track. As long as folks are talking about responding to the incident, it's all good. However, once you have accomplished all your objectives, I wouldn't suggest holding folks for the sake of using all the time. Their time is valuable. If you've accomplished your objectives, respect their time and let them go.

Also, I always provide lunch. People are busy and you really should give them that additional incentive to show up.

Invite your local FBI or Secret Service agent. If you take my advice from Chapter 3, you should be reaching out to your local (FBI) InfraGard chapter, U.S. Secret Service Electronic Crimes Task Force, and/ or regional cyber-crime task force. I've had an FBI agent show up for my annual tests. They provide an incredible perspective on what is really going on out there with cyber-crime. The question-and-answer sessions are invaluable. I really believe that the first time you meet your local law enforcement resource shouldn't be when you're overwhelmed in a crisis. I also think this is good for the agent/officer because it gives them some "inside" perspective on how the organizations in their jurisdiction are planning to react to crisis.

You should maintain all the records I described above. This is where that last section on records retention becomes important. You never know when you may need to demonstrate to an auditor, or as part of a civil lawsuit, that you have taken your responsibility seriously.

Like I said in the beginning of this chapter, the amount of focus you direct toward maintaining the relevance of your plans will pay large dividends when the call comes and you have to respond to crisis.

Plan Development: Malware

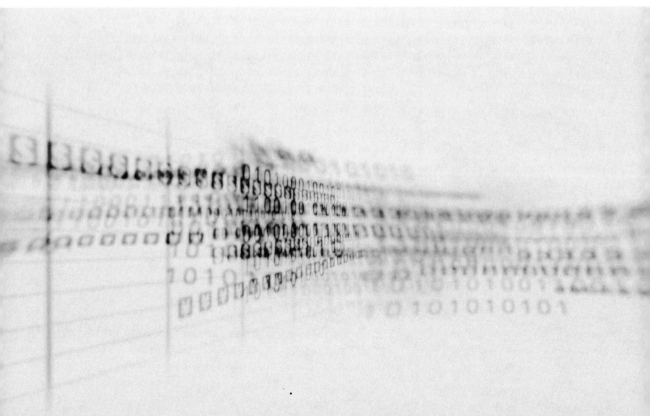

Your Malware Outbreak CIRP: Incident Preparation

s I mentioned in Chapters 4 and 5, your table of contents is the framework
of your plan. The table of contents shown next is for the Malware Outbreak
CIRP.

As you can see, this is pretty similar to the table of contents for the Data Breach plan in terms of format. But as we progress through the next three chapters, you will see that a Malware Outbreak plan is very different. I use the same foreword as the Data Breach plan, but the Advisory Committee has a very different composition.

Foreword

A Plan Is Preparation Manifested

Sound Information Security Management principles suggest that all organizations entrusted to maintain the Confidentiality, Integrity, and Availability of sensitive data should incorporate Protective, Detective, and Corrective measures to ensure such a result. Planning is a corrective mechanism and should be part of any Information Security effort. For planning to be an effective corrective mechanism, it must provide a solid foundation as to its execution, with specific information so that participants are empowered with current and relevant knowledge, and yet be broad as to not constrict an organization's ability to respond to unforeseen events. Planning will rarely answer all the questions that come up during an incident, but it should provide a repository of thoughtful anticipation, collaboration, and research. Furthermore, to assure a plan's continued usefulness, it should be tested and updated on a regular basis. A plan's true value is measured by the relevance of the information and processes it provides at a time of crisis.

XYZ Information Security is grateful to the following individuals who participated as part of the CIRP (Malware) Advisory Committee and provided valuable insight into the development of this plan:

Jennifer Jones – Problem Management
David Jones – IT Service & Support
Justin Jones – Incident Coordination Center
Brian Jones – Data Center Operations
Carl Jones – Platform Services
Ann Jones – Business Relationship Management

Unlike the Data Breach CIRP, the Advisory Committee is mostly technical staff with one very important exception. When it comes to malware, I believe that amateurs talk vulnerabilities and threats, but professionals talk about consequences. The U.S. Department of Homeland Security's (DHS) definition of risk, as per its National Infrastructure Protection Plan (NIPP), is Risk = Vulnerability + Threat + Consequence. As you will see as we go through the next three chapters, vulnerability and risk are important, but understanding consequence within your organization is imperative.

The following is the introduction section of the Malware Outbreak CIRP and is similar in format to the Data Breach CIRP. However, you will see in certain areas that malware requires very different organization and prirorities.

Plan Introduction

Plan Objective

A collaboratively developed, documented, and validated plan that enables XYZ to immediately respond to a malware outbreak in a manner that demonstrates appropriate Due Diligence in order to protect the confidentiality, integrity, and availability of our systems; continue to provide quality products and services to our customers; maintain confidence in the XYZ brand; and ultimately preserve shareholder value.

Again, I believe it is important that your objective relate back to the benefits to the business, as discussed in Chapter 4. It is not enough to have identified vulnerabilities and threats. If you lack a consequence to the organization, then do you really have a crisis? In the plan objective, we link the potential for a malware outbreak to impact the company's ability to deliver to its customers. This could impact point of sale, and in a worst-case scenario you are unable to sell goods or provide the value that differentiates your organization in the marketplace. If the organization is unable to perform its "center of gravity" functions, this can have negative repercussions all the way up to the C-level executives of the corporation. I have also seen malware outbreaks that basically had little to no effect on the corporation. I am not suggesting that you ignore those instances, but just be mindful that your primary objective is to maintain the organization's center of gravity—or, simply put, ensure that your *cure* isn't worse than the *disease* you are responding to.

Plan Scope and Assumptions

The scope of this Computer Incident Response Plan (CIRP) is corrective action for a Malware Outbreak.

The following assumptions are applicable to this plan:

1. An "Outbreak" is defined as six or more malware occurrences within a 24-hour period.
2. External parties are not initially involved (law enforcement, etc.).

3. There is a single threat (w/ variants) exploiting a common vulnerability. Multiple threats occurring simultaneously are not specifically identified by the plan.

4. No sensitive (i.e., PCI) data has been compromised based on the malware.

5. This plan will be a living document, subject to regular updates and testing.

One of the key distinctions we make in this section is that we define an "outbreak" as six or more occurrences within a 24-hour period. This is something we reached with the advisory committee and the Field Services team. I was surprised to find out just how often we were dispatching technicians to repair infected systems.

Plan Execution and Command Topologies

This plan is based on the following topology:

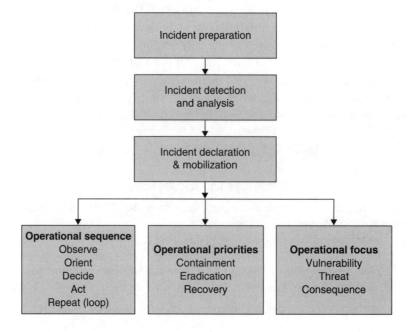

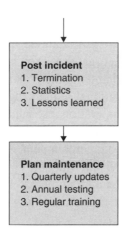

The CIRP (Malware) plan topology above delineates the manner in which this plan will address the preparatory, execution, and post event activities necessary to maintain and execute a planned response to malware outbreaks. The plan will detail three concurrent operational concepts: Sequence of execution (OODA), Priorities of effort, and Focus (division of labor).

During the execution of the plan, a management (command) topology is necessary to establish roles and responsibilities, ensure timely decision-making, and delineate boundaries to ensure effective utilization of resources.

The following topology should be followed for managing a major Malware outbreak incident:

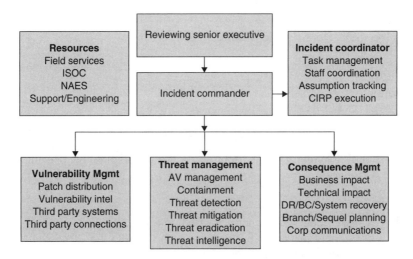

Greater discussion of these topologies will follow below.

Remember when I said earlier that a picture is worth a thousand words? The flowcharts shown in the preceding section are definitely worth that many words. The first illustrates how the plan is organized. You have preparation, detection, and declaration. As you will read in Chapter 9, the plan is organized around three major areas. The first is this idea of operational sequencing. Remember in the "conference call from Hell" in Chapter 1, that operational sequencing or "battle rhythm" was an absent component. The second area the plan will address is the text book responses to any sort of unauthorized intrusion: containment, eradication, and recovery. The third area is around this idea of division of labor. This is how you divide up the work so that work can be done in parallel and immediately resolve the crisis at hand. I took the DHS NIPP definition of risk and put it to work. Finally, there's post incident and maintenance considerations.

The second flowchart is probably the most interesting. During time of execution, this is the "who does what" picture. We'll discuss this in much greater detail in the next chapter. As with the data breach plan, these first pages are there to impress upon the new reader the level of detail that you invested in this plan and to provide them a preview at a high level of what awaits them in greater detail further in the plan.

Plan Ownership

The XYZ CISO (Suzie Queue) is the senior executive responsible for the development, maintenance, and execution of this plan.

This plan is managed by the Information Security Operations Center (ISOC).

The ISOC Plans Point of Contact (POC) is:

N. McCarthy
1 Busy St.
Northern, CA 94598
(925) 123-4567

Supporting Documentation

Additional documentation is required for the development & execution of this malware outbreak plan. Contained within this plan will be the following:

▶ **References** References are both internal XYZ and external documents that contain information pertinent to the successful execution of the XYZ CIRP.

► **Enclosures**   Enclosures are typically non-doctrinal documents that contain useful information. Diagrams, spreadsheets, etc., are typically considered as enclosures. Enclosures are usually information relevant to the task at hand, but not maintained or controlled by the author of this plan.

► **Tabs**   Tabs are specific items of information, relevant to the plan, but containing perishable data for which there is no other source. Tabs may typically include information such as Point of Contact data. Tab data will be located both within the text of the plan to support the flow of the document and in the appendix for quick access.

► **Restricted Information**   Restricted information is required for the execution of this plan and could be used by unauthorized individuals to the detriment of XYZ or its customers. References to restricted data in this document must be identified as such and will normally contain a link to the internal XYZ ShareIT site and will be password protected. Access to Restricted information will be managed by the ISOC.

► **Hyperlinks**   All references, enclosures, and tabs will be hyperlinked throughout the document for immediate access. A network connection is required to take advantage of this capability. Should this document be shared outside of XYZ, hardcopy versions will be needed for any of the supporting documentation.

The following are the references, enclosures, and tabs for this plan:

Ref: (1) NIST Computer Security Incident Handling Guide (Special Pub 800-61 Jan 2004)

(2) XYZ Malware Mitigation Process April 2008

(3) US Army Field Manual 101-5 Staff Organization and Operations

Encl: (1) Third-Party Security Inc. Incident Response Retainer SOW

Tab: (A) Isolation Points within the XYZ Enterprise **RESTRICTED**

(B) Business Impact overlay of isolation points **RESTRICTED**

(C) ISOC Threat Portfolio **RESTRICTED**

(F) Incident Notification POCs

(G) Key Resource Escalation/Back-up Instruction **RESTRICTED**

Updating and Synchronization

The information contained within this plan is only valuable as long as it is relevant. The objective of maintaining current information in a plan is to ensure that at time of immediate execution, the plan provides relevant information to ensure successful execution. To this end, it is incumbent upon those tasked with maintaining this plan to confirm the currency of the references, enclosures, and tabs listed above.

Document	Last Verification	Responsible Party
Ref (1) NIST Guide	2/25/08	ISOC
Ref (2) XYZ Malware Mitigation SOP	2/10/11	Field Services
Ref (3) US Army Field Manual 101-5 Staff Organization and Operations	2/10/11	ISOC
Encl (1) Third Party Services Inc Emergency Response Subscription Services SOW (w/ POC info)	11/12/11	ISOC
Tab (A) Isolation Points within the XYZ Enterprise	2/15/12	Network Engineering
Tab (B) Business Impact Overlay of Tab (A)	2/15/12	Retail Portfolio Management
Tab (C) ISOC Threat Portfolio	6/01/11	ISOC
Tab (F) Incident Notification POC's	11/12/11	ISOC
Tab (G) Key Resource Escalation/Back-up Instruction	10/26/11	ISOC

Additional information regarding the maintenance of this plan is contained in the Plan Maintenance section listed below.

Much like the Data Breach CIRP, the materials listed in the preceding section will be described in greater detail in the following section.

Incident Preparation

The purpose of this section of the plan is to ensure that adequate information regarding the XYZ environment is immediately available in the event of a computer incident. This information must be verified on a regular basis to ensure its relevancy/accuracy.

Isolation Points within the XYZ Enterprise

Isolation Points (also called "Choke Points") within the XYZ Enterprise (Tab A) details the various locations within the network where a containment action could be taken to prevent the spread of a virus. This document is XYZ RESTRICTED. The disclosure of this document to unauthorized parties may cause serious risk to XYZ. This document is currently in development and could be made available in draft form during an incident.

Business Impact Overlay of Isolation Points

The "Business Impact Overlay" document (Tab B) details the potential business impact for any containment actions taken using the "Isolation Points within the XYZ Enterprise" (Tab A). This document is XYZ RESTRICTED. The disclosure of this document to unauthorized parties may cause serious risk to XYZ. This document is currently in development and could be made available in draft form during an incident.

ISOC Threat Portfolio

The "ISOC Threat Portfolio" (Tab C) details those known systems within the enterprise with vulnerabilities that will not be remediated in the near term. The ISOC provides other compensating controls to help mitigate risks to these systems. These systems are included in the CIRP as possible likely avenues of exploitation within the environment. This document is XYZ RESTRICTED. The disclosure of this document to unauthorized parties may cause serious risk to XYZ.

One of the first documents we have is a containment plan. Containment is definitely one of those "easier said than done" topics. The idea is that when you have an outbreak, and you have no idea how it's spreading or what it's doing to the machines it's infecting, containment becomes one of your most important decisions. One of the last modern engineering marvels that lacked an adequate containment mechanism was the *Titanic*. Too many people think they can just wing it. Containment is the chief engineering/technical response to the "fog of war." It's exactly when you have no idea how something is spreading, or what it's doing to the infected system, that you have to look at containment.

One other concept that's been coming up in discussions lately is this idea of functional versus geographic containment. Let me explain. What we have in this plan is really geared toward geographic containment. There's a virus in Asia and we don't want it to spread to North America. The containment action is to sever the corporate link to Asia. The other concept is starting to gain a lot more traction is about functional containment. What's driving this is the proliferation of all these handheld PDAs and laptops. We have so much "attack surface" outside of our normal perimeter that we've started discussing the idea of a "functional containment." Say, for example, we have a major global virus outbreak. One of the first areas we may want to isolate until we understand more about how the virus works is all those remote systems "dialing in" to the corporate network from home or other non-corporate locations. Cut off the iPads, remote connect laptops, and so on, from logging in (possibly infected) until we can master this problem.

The third dimension that, in all honesty, we haven't had the time or focus to start addressing is third-party connections. There's another set of points you may want to look at closing off once you get infected. Again, this is much easier said than done. One other comment on containment: it's not permanent. You may want to "contain" for a couple of hours to see how things work out. Again, this is not an easy answer to the problem.

But this brings up the second point of consideration that also happens to be the second document. What about the impact of the containment? Or, simply, will the cure be worse than the disease? This is where that focus on consequence is really so important to responding to this type of crisis. What we've done is to perform a basic business impact analysis on the containment points to determine what would be the business impact if we isolated that part of the business. This does a couple of things. First, it helps in making that decision to isolate. You now have an idea of how bad the cure is relative to the disease. The second is that it also now gives you a listing of those groups or functions that will be impacted. Hopefully, they have a sound business continuity plan, but at a minimum you can reach out to them and let them know what's going on and why.

The third point of consideration is what our ISOC calls the "threat portfolio." In the textbook, vulnerabilities are patched and everyone lives happily ever after. However, that isn't what always happens out in the real world. Businesses, especially large businesses, have older systems that aren't necessarily compatible with the latest patches. Or the code that needs to be patched is part of a combination of applications/software that can't be updated without impacting some other typically older code. So it is not uncommon to have older programs out there with known vulnerabilities that will not be patched anytime soon. If this is the case with your infrastructure, you should maintain a listing of those systems and apply other measures to protect them. These are vulnerable systems and are some of the first systems you should consider when you have a malware outbreak. The flip-side is that some of these vulnerabilities are so old that nobody is writing viruses for them. At a minimum, you should know where you are most vulnerable.

Third-Party Support Services

PCI Forensics Investigator (PFI)

As part of the PCI requirements for XYZ, Third-Party Services Inc. is currently contracted to provide Incident Response Services through the ISOC. In the event of a malware outbreak, specific third-party services could be necessary to meet either operational or obligatory requirements. The hyperlink below links you to the SOW for the Third-Party Services Inc. service. This service has been prepaid and on retainer through August 31 of 2012.

BXD LongSight Threat Management System

The BXD LongSight Threat Management System is an online repository of current threat information. XYZ (InfoSec) currently holds a license to access the information maintained in order to develop threat intelligence and find recommendations to remediate a malware outbreak. This service is available via the ISOC.

We leverage our PCI third-party support as a possible resource. If things get out of hand and we need resources to assist us, they may be an option. Also, because we have so many different technology platforms, we utilize a threat intelligence service. These services are very helpful in identifying the various vulnerabilities for many different technology platforms. I list both of these resources in the plan since they can potentially be resources to help deal with an incident. However, my experience has been that during these zero-day outbreaks, they're initially as clueless as the rest of us.

Incident Detection, Analysis, and Declaration

Sources of Precursors and Indicators

Listed below are potential sources of data breach detection available to XYZ Inc.:

ISOC Monitoring Feeds

The ISOC currently monitors systems throughout the enterprise resulting in upwards of 14 million events a day. Some of these events can be indicators of possible or likely malware activity and will initiate an investigation from the ISOC.

Field Services Responding to Malware Calls

On any given day, malicious programs such as viruses, spyware, Trojan horses, etc. (collectively referred to as malware for this document), will disrupt someone's productivity. Although most malware incidents are benign, the ISOC, Desktop Services, and Field Services have promulgated the XYZ Malware Mitigation Process (Reference 6). This SOP makes first responders aware that malware can be used as a tool to penetrate the XYZ network and defines specific steps that are to be taken should an occurrence of malware be identified as being a threat to XYZ. Per this SOP, Desktop Services and Field Services personnel will notify the ISOC of six or more Malware incidents that occur in a 24-hour period involving the same malware (exploit).

NOC, Service Desk, and Other Internal Sources of Detection

It is not always obvious when a malware outbreak has occurred. Often, other anomalies within the enterprise may serve as possible indicators of an outbreak. Activities such as unusual network traffic, increased CPU utilization on a device, and other questionable activity may be suspect and should be taken seriously. Whenever these types of incidents/tickets become known by other support entities within XYZ, the ISOC should be contacted so a thorough investigation of the situation can occur.

The following are signs that you may have a malware outbreak:

► Unknown or unexpected outgoing Internet traffic
► Unknown or unexpected network traffic from store and headquarter locations
► Unknown or unexpected services and applications configured to launch automatically on system boot
► Anti-virus programs malfunctioning or becoming disabled for unknown reasons
► Degraded processing capability (increased CPU utilization)

The major point to be made here is that there are many possible sources of detecting a malware infection. Typically, it is some non-ISOC source that first notifies us that something is going on that appears to be unusual and/or malicious.

Incident Threshold

Not all discoveries of malware constitute a malware outbreak. XYZ on a daily basis responds to suspected and confirmed malware infections. Per the Malware SOP (Ref 2), a malware outbreak is defined as six or more Malware incidents occurring in a 24-hour period involving the same malware (exploit).

Incident Analysis

The initial impact analysis of a malware outbreak is an essential task in order to effectively mobilize the appropriate technical and business resources. Impact analysis also helps provide an initial estimation as to the scope of the malware outbreak. When determining the initial impact of a suspected outbreak, it may not be possible to have all the necessary information prior to making an impact determination. It is critical during any assessment of potential impact not only to identify the source and credibility of the information you are using, but also to be forthcoming with the information you do not have and identify any assumptions that were necessary to complete your analysis.

Technical Impact

The technical impact analysis is where the scope of the malware outbreak is identified to specific data storage, processing, and transportation technologies. If possible, the more detail, the better. Version numbers, IP addresses, etc., all are beneficial when identifying the necessary resources that need to be mobilized.

At a minimum, the technical impact analysis should contain:

1. What system(s) have been affected?
2. Has any data been compromised?
3. What IT services are being impacted?
4. How did the malware gain access?
5. What vulnerability or service is being exploited?
6. How widespread is that vulnerability or service within XYZ?

7. Were we able to detect this incident with our current ISOC tools?

8. Is there a means available to prevent the malware from spreading?

9. Is there a mechanism to eradicate the malware currently available?

Business Impact

1. Is public or personnel safety affected?

2. How many customers may be affected by this incident?

3. What products/goods/services does this outbreak affect?

4. Has XYZ lost the ability to control/record/measure/track any significant amounts of inventory/products/cash/revenue?

5. Is there any indication that this act would be exploited for malicious or criminal activity?

6. Who currently knows about this incident (inside and outside of XYZ)?

7. What is the worst-case business impact if XYZ is unable to mitigate this outbreak?

I sat down with one of the field services managers and we came up with the six or more malware events per day that trigger a malware outbreak. This is what we determined as appropriate for our organization. Your organization may set this higher or lower. The key is that you have worked out a mutually agreed boundary as to when you have a malware incident and when is it business as usual.

The next section details the process to notify resources and mobilize folks for a malware outbreak.

Incident Declaration

The formal declaration of a malware outbreak should not be taken lightly and will require the approval of a manager on the CIRP response team. Accurate reporting in the initial stages of an incident is critical to ensure the proper mobilization of resources necessary to deal with the incident.

When a malware outbreak is initially suspected, an Initial Incident Notification message will be sent out. Once there is probable cause to suspect malware is infecting the enterprise, the Computer Incident Declaration will be distributed in accordance with this plan.

Incident Notification and Mobilization

Initial Incident Notification is the process of notifying relevant parties of a possible outbreak that is currently under investigation. The initial notification should contain the following information:

COMPUTER INCIDENT NOTIFICATION
The parties listed below are investigating a POSSIBLE malware outbreak.

Date/time:

Incident coordinator POC:

Approving manager POC:

Source of detection/notification:

Outbreak characteristics:

Technical impact:

Business impact:

Next Steps:

- Confirmation/Denial of outbreak:

- Obstacles (if any):

Next update and Means:

End of Message

Incident Declaration is the process of notifying relevant parties once a conclusion has been made that there is probable cause to believe that a malware outbreak is currently infecting XYZ. This declaration does not require complete knowledge of the circumstances of the outbreak, but sufficient evidence that would cause a prudent person to believe an outbreak is occurring. An incident declaration needs to contain the following information:

COMPUTER INCIDENT DECLARATION – MALWARE OUTBREAK
You are being notified that a MALWARE OUTBREAK IS OCCURRING and XYZ resources will be required to support this incident.

Incident summary:

Technical impact:

Business impact:

Coordination conference call to be held at:
Date
Time
Call in number
Passcode

Incident coordinator POC:

Approving manager POC:

Refer to the following items for additional information:

1. The initial Incident Notification is attached to provide more details regarding the incident and efforts prior to making this declaration.

2. In order to access the XYZ Computer Incident Response Plan (CIRP) for Malware Outbreaks, refer to the internal XYZ ShareIT site:
http://collab.XYZ.com/it/cirp/Malware%20CIRP/Forms/AllItems.aspx

3. Access to XYZ RESTRICTED documents pertaining to the CIRP are also on the ShareIT site but are password protected to pre-authorized parties. Contact the ISOC at InfoSec.Operations@XYZ.com in order to have your name added to the access roster.

End of Message

Below are the minimum expectations as to incident notification and mobilization:

Group	POC	Role	
CISO	Suzy Queue	Reviewing Senior Involved Executive	
Service and Support	David Jones	Incident Commander	Involved
Incident Coordination Center	Cheryl Jones	Incident Coordinator	Involved
ISOC	Neal Jones	Threat Manager	Involved
Service and Support	Ann Jones	Consequence Manager	Involved
Desktop Mobile Engineering (AV)	Kevin Jones	Vulnerability Manager	Involved
InfoSec Engineering	Armando Jones	Resource	Informed
Network Architecture, Engineering & Support	Phillip Jones	Resource	Informed
XYZ Forensics	Suzanne Jones	Resource	Informed
Desktop Mobile Engineering	Mike Jones	Resource	Informed
Software Delivery Group	Larry Jones	Resource	Informed
Web Services	Nick Jones	Resource	Informed
Disaster Recovery/Business Continuity	Pat Jones	Resource	Informed
Data Center Operations	Wil Jones	Resource	Informed
Field Services	Lynn Jones	Resource	Informed
Change Management	Dianne Jones	Resource	Informed
Platform Services	Henry Jones	Resource	Informed
Central LAN	Doug Jones	Resource	As Required

Tab (F) "Incident Notification POCs" contains contact information for all parties that may be involved in a malware response. Tab (G) "Key Resource Escalation/Back-up Instruction" **RESTRICTED** is also available in the event key individuals are not accessible using the normal notification process. The "Incident Notification POC" Tab (F) contains contact information for all individuals that may be called into a response and is not the listing of all individuals to notify in case of a malware outbreak.

~~I A M-IPH-HUM-IDU C.N. H. TA~~

As with the Data Breach CIRP, I recommend a consistent format for notifying parties of a malware incident. Finally, you should make every effort to document your efforts when responding to a malware incident.

~~I A M-IPH-HUM-IDU C.N. H. TA~~

Incident Documentation

Documentation serves a key role in responding to any incident. The ability to capture, distribute, and store detailed information regarding the efforts made responding to an incident are key to an efficient response, lessons learned, and post-event concerns. Time permitting, all participants should maintain a detailed log/journal of time spent, actions taken, and additional involved parties starting from the initial notification/detection through the termination of the event.

~~I A M-IPH-HUM-IDU C.N. H. TA~~

This concludes the Malware Outbreak CIRP incident preparation chapter. Again, this is what we have come up with for our organization. Hopefully, you can leverage this to develop a CIRP that works for your organization. The next chapter will take us into crisis.

Your Malware Outbreak
CIRP: Plan Execution

A malware crisis is one of the most difficult incidents to deal with. You have an active "agent" competing against you. It has the element of surprise and it has the initiative. If it is a zero-day, most of your defenses are useless. Little knowledge regarding this opponent is readily available. You have to make quick decisions with little information. There are few resources that you can reach out to for help, because they too are reacting to what is going on.

I believe that malware is going to change for the worse. I firmly believe that we will soon enter an era in which malware becomes a much more destructive entity than ever before.

Plan Execution

No plan is ever perfect. However, at a time of heightened activity and anxiety, having a consistent expectation among diverse parties, each with unique perspectives but with a shared objective, is invaluable. One of the objectives of this CIRP is to establish that consistent expectation as to the method of how XYZ Inc. will respond to a malware outbreak. The first expectation will be describing the roles and organization of the various principals to the execution of this plan. The second section will discuss common activities during an incident and recommend a repeatable timeline for their execution.

Organization and Roles

During the execution of the CIRP, six major components of the response will need to perform simultaneously. Based on the concept that Risk = Vulnerability + Threat + Consequence, there will be six functional roles within this CIRP: Review, Command, Coordination, Vulnerability, Threat, and Consequence. These are all necessary functions, occurring simultaneously in times of great stress and confusion. It is imperative that all involved in the CIRP understand what is expected of them and the other members of the team. Greater detail for each of these roles is provided below.

The descriptions provided below are for a major incident possibly involving numerous resources with XYZ. In the event of a minor event, the roles provided may be combined/collapsed, but the same basic functions are required to execute the CIRP.

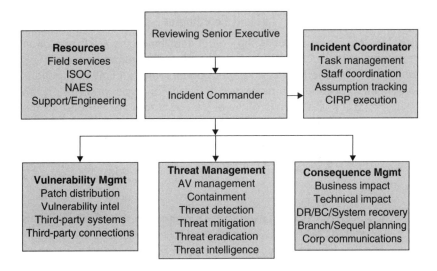

Incident Commander

The Incident Commander will ultimately be responsible for meeting the overall success of the response effort. The Incident Commander must be empowered by the corporation to be capable of making timely decisions when necessary. During times of disagreement, the Incident Commander will need to be formally apprised of the circumstances and presented with options, and he/she will need to determine the best course of action under the time constraints that are in effect. The Incident Commander must be informed of the current efforts and will be responsible for status reports to senior management within XYZ. The Incident Commander is also responsible for identifying and engaging the Reviewing Senior Executive.

Reviewing Senior Executive

It is imperative during a crisis that impartial management oversight is available to protect the interests of XYZ. By not being directly involved in the incident response, the Reviewing Senior Executive is able to remain informed yet emotionally detached. Secondly, when the Incident Commander is busy with the immediate execution of the CIRP, the Reviewing Senior Executive can provide a common point of focus for other senior executives who may have concerns with the incident response. Finally, the Reviewing Senior Executive is best suited to determine if the current response is adequate and may direct additional resources, elevate the priority within XYZ, or direct more senior/capable leadership of the task force. The Reviewing Senior Executive should not become directly involved in the response unless it is to assume the role of the Incident Commander.

Incident Coordinator

The Incident Coordinator is the "glue" that holds the CIRP execution together. Typically, the Incident Coordinator will be either from the ISOC or the ICC. Prior to the declaration of an incident, a number of actions are taken to prepare the plan, and to detect, analyze, and declare an incident. Upon the mobilization of the resources to respond to the incident, a turnover briefing will be necessary to bring all parties to the same level of understanding regarding both the malware outbreak and the CIRP. During the execution of the CIRP, the Incident Coordinator will need to drive the execution of the plan. This includes the following functions:

▶ **CIRP Execution**   Ensuring that all mechanisms of the CIRP are working as planned or changed as necessary. Roles are assigned, and the defined segregation of duties is being followed.

▶ **Task Management**   In support of the Incident Commander, tracking all tasks assigned within the malware outbreak task force and ensures timely completion.

▶ **Staff Coordination**   Includes setting up meetings, organizing decision and status briefs, and ensuring timely attendance and maintaining meeting notes.

▶ **Assumption Tracking**   During fluid events such as a malware outbreak, where information is not always available (the fog of war), assumptions must be made to facilitate timely decision-making. These assumptions need to be tracked and constantly validated. Once sufficient information is available and an assumption can be deemed to be factual, it should no longer be tracked. If an assumption is deemed to be faulty, then immediate adjustments must be made to the current effort.

Subordinate to the Incident Commander are three functional managers. The three functional areas identified in this plan are based on the concept that Risk = Vulnerability + Threat + Consequence ("risk triad"). The three functional areas will cut across many of the normal day-to-day organizational structures. Managers of potential resources such as Field Services, Server Operations, ISOC, etc., should expect to be tasked from each of these three functional managers.

Vulnerability Manager

Vulnerabilities are typically the basis upon which malware (threats) function. Vulnerabilities are manifested in many forms. Improper coding techniques that create opportunities for the unintended use of installed programs are one such vulnerability. As these programming errors are discovered, the manufacturer usually releases "patch" information to remedy these deficiencies. Vulnerabilities can also manifest in the form of unintended services/features being made available by devices on the network. Within XYZ, hardening standards are provided to reduce the availability of these vulnerabilities. Often the best mechanism to prevent a malware outbreak is to eliminate any vulnerability that may be exploited by unwanted parties.

The Vulnerability Manager will focus his/her efforts on the vulnerability portion of the risk triad. The Vulnerability Manager is responsible for knowing where the vulnerability exists within the XYZ managed enterprise. The Vulnerability Manager is also responsible for identifying those third-party systems and network connections that could also be conduits for the threat (e.g., worm) to spread. The Vulnerability Manager is also responsible for the patch management effort to remove the vulnerability associated with the rapidly spreading malware.

The Vulnerability Manager shall task, as necessary, any resources that will assist in discovering and remediating the exploited vulnerability. Subfunctional areas include the following:

- ► Patch distribution
- ► Vulnerability scans
- ► Configuration scans
- ► Identification of third-party systems
- ► Identification or third-party network connections
- ► Coordination with third-party support personnel
- ► Containment/isolation of third-party systems and connections (external to the enterprise)

Threat Manager

The second leg of the malware risk triad is the threat (malware). Much like any other computer program, malware has unique characteristics that need to be understood and exploited to minimize and/or defeat it. The Threat Manager is tasked with mitigating the malware threat. This is accomplished through several concurrent actions. First and foremost, the Threat Manager must discover and maintain all available information on the threat itself. This information includes the following:

▶ What function(s) does the malware perform on the infected machine(s)?

▶ How is this a threat to XYZ?

▶ How does the malware propagate within the environment?

▶ Does the malware initially arrive ready to perform its intended purpose, or is there a "maturation" process it needs to follow to become fully effective, and can this process be interrupted in order to prevent the threat from reaching full maturity/capability?

▶ What signatures/indicators will assist in detecting the threat?

▶ What tools/processes/resources within XYZ are able to detect, contain/isolate, mitigate, or eradicate the threat?

The Threat Manager must address the following concerns:

▶ **Anti-virus management** Is the XYZ AV solution able to protect uninfected systems and remediate infected systems effectively? Working with the Vulnerability Manager, identify possible gaps where an AV solution will not be sufficient.

▶ **Containment/isolation** Identify actions that can be taken to deny the threats ability to propagate within the enterprise.

▶ **Threat detection** Identify signatures/indicators that can be used to identify both the presence of the threat within the environment, and also provide information as to the capability ("maturity") of the threat. Work with resources to monitor for new infections.

▶ **Threat mitigation** Identify opportunities that may prevent the threat from reaching its fullest capability or otherwise neutralize the threat from producing consequences within the environment.

▶ **Threat eradication** How do we remove the threat from infected machines?

▶ **Threat intelligence** Do we have the most current information on the threat on an ongoing basis?

Consequence Manager

The third leg of the malware risk triad is the consequence (impact) created by the threat exploiting a vulnerability. Consequence is the critical component of assessing the relevance of a malware outbreak to the organization. The role of Consequence Manager is also the most forward-looking of the three and is primarily concerned with both current and potential impact brought on by the malware to the business of XYZ. The Consequence Manager must also provide sufficient consideration to future planning for the corporation in the event current efforts are insufficient. This planning should focus primarily on business impact. The consequence manager must be mindful of the following:

► Primarily focused on business impact
  ► Current and potential
  ► From the malware (threat)
  ► From those actions taken to address the malware (cure worse than disease)
  ► In business terms
    ► Ability to provide goods and services to customers
    ► Ability to track/record/account for assets
    ► Confidentiality, Integrity, Availability of business information
    ► Brand impact
    ► Statutory and contractual business obligations
      ► Notifications, service outages, PCI
► Technical impact
  ► Current and potential
  ► From the malware (threat)
  ► From those actions taken to address the malware (cure worse than disease)
► Consequence mitigation—efforts to prevent, reduce, remediate, or tolerate the effects of the outbreak impacting critical business processes
  ► Disaster recovery plans & resources
  ► Business continuity plans

- ▶ Availability of "fallback" capability
  - ▶ Store and forward
  - ▶ Manual processes
  - ▶ Limited services/functionality
  - ▶ Duration limitations
- ▶ System recovery efforts of critical systems
  - ▶ Prioritization
  - ▶ Aggregation
- ▶ Containment considerations
  - ▶ Quarantine/localization of outbreak
    - ▶ To contain effect (consequence)
    - ▶ To tolerate (co-exist with) an infected environment while performing business functions
  - ▶ Business impact of containment
  - ▶ Business risk of not containing the outbreak
- ▶ Corporate communications
  - ▶ Notices to employees
  - ▶ Notices to management
  - ▶ Notices to third parties
- ▶ Branch / Sequel planning
  - ▶ Current actions aren't sufficient/successful
  - ▶ Conceptual development of "Plan B"
  - ▶ Conceptual development of "what next" plan (2+ planning cycles ahead)
  - ▶ Constantly focused on the business impact
  - ▶ Mindful of the worst case scenario

The roles described above are recommended for a major malware outbreak in which there may be many involved parties and envisions individuals from within XYZ filling each defined role. For less significant events, these roles may be combined into one or two people for execution. The size of the task force and its ability to accommodate all the various involved parties/responsibilities effectively will determine if these roles should be consolidated.

As I mentioned, your plan should be narrative in nature. Participants of the plan will most likely lack the familiarity with the plan that you have as its author. It is imperative that they be able to pick up your plan and read everything they need to know to be successful. Once you have the appropriate structure established, your next step is to establish a common expectation as the ad hoc organization's *battle rhythm*. This is especially important when you have to allow for parallel actions and ensure that there is sufficient time for members of the team to get the work done. As the tension increases, you need to ensure that there is sufficient discipline established within your plan.

Operational Sequencing

In the execution of this plan, participants should not only be able to anticipate "what comes next," but should be provided sufficient guidance and time to perform those functions necessary to respond to a malware outbreak. The following is the anticipated process for a malware outbreak:

- ▶ Initiation phase (one-time)
    - ▶ Initial incident notification
    - ▶ Initial incident declaration
    - ▶ Initial coordination conference call
        - ▶ Designation of six functional roles (Review, Command, Coordination, Vulnerability, Threat, and Consequence)
        - ▶ Formal assignment/allocation / commitment of resources
        - ▶ Establishment of reporting (execution) cycle
        - ▶ Additional notification/mobilization
- ▶ Incident resolution phase (recurring basis)
    - ▶ Conduct Status Brief with malware outbreak task force management
        - ▶ Not to exceed 25 percent of the execution cycle to ensure sufficient opportunity to execute tasks
        - ▶ Provide decision briefs as required to the Incident Commander
        - ▶ Incident Commander makes decision(s) and assigns tasks

> ▶ Manage assigned resources and complete assigned tasks
>
> ▶ OODA cycle repeats until the incident is resolved

▶ Incident termination phase (one time)

> ▶ Decision to terminate incident
>
> ▶ Lessons learned submission(s)
>
> ▶ Incident metrics reporting

The frequency with which you repeat this loop can be measured by the frequency with which you do your status briefs. If you are going to have a status brief every two hours, then you need to ensure that there is sufficient time for resources to be able to work on their tasks. In a two-hour cycle, I would suggest no more than 30 minutes for the status brief, leaving 90 minutes for actual work to get done.

Your next consideration is what you do with the resources you have. The following is from the plan and describes your priorities.

Operational Priorities

The textbook solution (NIST Computer Security Incident Handling Guide [Special Pub 800-61]):

▶ Prioritize the handling of the incident based on its business impact (consequence)

▶ Containment takes priority over eradication and recovery

▶ Protect the following first whenever possible (in order of priority):

> ▶ Retail Stores
>
> ▶ PCI Systems
>
> ▶ Data Centers
>
> ▶ Distribution Centers
>
> ▶ Corp Leadership
>
> ▶ Corp Headquarters

The next section of the plan talks about tools and resources available to help you respond to a malware crisis. Obviously, your organization will have technical resources. You need to ensure that when a malware crisis is declared those resources are on the call and working for one of the three functional managers, as described within the CIRP. We also discussed the "Battle Rhythm" of the malware response. Two things will need to happen on a regular basis: One is the *status brief*. This is critical to ensure everyone on the team is aware of what's going on. The next section will discuss the *status brief* within the CIRP, and I will provide more discussion of the *status brief* I use later in the chapter. The other thing you will need to do when your management meets is to be able to make timely decisions.

One of the tools you may want to consider is the *decision brief*. You will need a format, a mechanism to present options and empower a decision. The PowerPoint brief may be too cumbersome to meet your Battle Rhythm, but it is something for you to consider. At a minimum, you can use it as a sort of discussion template.

Operational Resources

The functional managers (vulnerability, threat, and consequence) task resources to serve the needs of the incident response. Resources will most likely be tasked by all three of the functional managers during the Initial Coordination Conference call. Additional tasking should be expected during the entire incident response effort. It is the responsibility of the appropriate resource manager to clarify and prioritize the tasks assigned to their respective resources and seek guidance from the Incident Commander when conflicts arise. The Resource Manager is ultimately responsible for the services they provide the functional manager(s).

Synchronization and Decision-Making

Listed below are predefined templates for both decision and status briefs to be provided to the Incident Commander on a regular basis in the event of a malware outbreak.

Status Reports

The human cognitive process has been defined by some as the process of Observation, Orientation, Decision, and Action (OODA). For operational staffs, this process needs to repeat itself on a regular basis so that the task force is able to effectively evaluate and execute an actionable response to a crisis on an ongoing basis until the crisis is resolved. A key component of this OODA process is the *status brief*. The utilization of a cyclically scheduled status brief, which ensures sufficient time within the reporting cycle for the task force to execute assigned tasks, is the backbone of an operational response methodology.

All regular status updates given during the execution of the Malware CIRP should use the dedicated Malware Status Brief PowerPoint slide deck. Each of the functional managers will update and present their respective slides during the status brief. This will ensure a more disciplined discussion and a more efficient exchange of information. These slides will also be posted to a shared location, where all members of the task force and other interested parties can view a summary of the status.

The following rules apply when presenting during a status brief:

1. Operational briefings are intended to be concise but comprehensive.

2. The longer you take talking about what needs to be done, the less time you have to actually do it.

3. Do not read your slides; your slides should be self-explanatory.

4. Highlight new information in red. Most of the presentation is repeated information.

5. Be immediately available for questions when asked.

6. Slides will be posted and available to everyone.

7. A brief where all that you hear is "next slide please" is a GOOD brief.

8. Submit your slides prior to the brief so the organizer of the meeting has sufficient time.

Decision Briefs

The objective of any operational response is to ensure the timely execution of actions. Often during high tempo, high stress operational events, a decision is needed that either cannot be reached through consensus within the task force, or is of a serious enough impact that it should be made only by the Incident Commander. It is the role of the staff to prepare the Incident Commander to make this decision. The Malware Decision Brief PowerPoint deck should be used whenever a decision needs to be made by the Incident Commander.

The following guidelines should be followed whenever making a decision brief:

1. The purpose of a decision brief is to empower the Incident Commander.
2. Provide a thorough discussion of the pros and cons of the various possible decisions.
3. Examine ALL the options available, including not making a decision.
4. Do not let personal bias limit your presentation. Your role is to provide the Incident Commander with sufficient information to make their decision, not to convince them of your inclination.

I cannot emphasize enough the value I gained from leveraging these PowerPoint tools with the malware CIRP team. The goal of these slides is two-fold. Firstly, to ensure you are discussing all the *relevant* topics. Secondly, that you are only covering the relevant topics *briefly*.

Especially with malware, since so much is not known at the time of execution, the fog of war and friction can almost become overwhelming. One of the means of keeping the discussion on target and on task is by enforcing the structure of the slides. For example, when the vulnerability slide is up, only the Vulnerability Manager speaks to the issues. And when that slide is done, you move on to the next slide/topic. If people in the audience disagree or have a concern, instead of bogging down the entire team with speculative concerns, the individual(s) with concerns should be directed to reach out the owner of that slide and discuss the issue off-line. Again, the goal is to move through the slides, present the information, make decisions, and take action.

Listed below is the Malware Status Brief.

> **Malware Outbreak**
> Status Brief
> of
> 12 Nov 2011/1300 MST

Status Brief Outline

• Updates:
- Malware response assignments
- Vulnerability-threat-consequence updates
- Previously assigned tasks & assumptions
• Next steps (efforts)
• Incident Commander's input
• Next status brief
• Execute

Status Brief Guidance

• Presenters, do not read your slides to the audience – if your audience cannot read, we're in big trouble. If you have to explain all your slides, you're in big trouble.
• The longer you take talking about what needs to be done, the less time you have to actually do it.
• New entries in red, repeat info in black.
• Slides will be posted and available to everyone.
• A brief where all that you hear is "next slide please" is a GOOD brief.
• Get your slides in at least 15 min prior to the next brief.

Assigned Roles

• Incident Commander: Charles Jones
• Reviewing Senior Executive: Dan Jones
• Incident Coordinator: John Jones
• Vulnerability Manager: Carl Jones
• Threat Manager: Mike Jones
• Consequence Manager: Ann Jones

Vulnerability Update

- Exploited Vulnerability:
- Patch/remediation info:
- Corrected systems:
- Vulnerable Systems:
- Vulnerable third-party systems:
- Third-party network connections:

Threat Update

- Description of threat:
  - What does it do?
  - How does it work/mature?
- XYZ Corp AV Status:
- Threat signatures/indicators:
- Additional Info on the threat:
- Threat info is current as of:

Consequence Update

- Current business impact of threat:
- Current technical impact of threat:
- Current business impact of response:
- Current technical impact of response:
- Probable business impact with current approach:
- Any significant business concerns:

Previously Assigned Tasks

- Task title – assigned to – due
- Determine patch level of CCTV – Jones – 4/5/1300 MST

Current Assumptions

- Summary – assigned to
- Blocking port 445 will prevent propagation of threat – Mike Jones

Planning Guidance

- From the textbook
  - Prioritize the handling of the incident based on its business impact (consequence).
  - Containment takes priority over eradication and recovery.

Vulnerability Mgmt Efforts

• Tasks necessary to remediate vulnerability

• Are current efforts sufficient

• Next steps

• Issues/roadblocks

Threat Mgmt Efforts

• Tasks necessary to remediate threat

–Propagation

–Mitigation

–Detection

–Eradication

• Are the current efforts sufficient

• Next steps

• Issues/Roadblocks

Consequence Mgmt Efforts

• Current efforts to reduce/mitigate effects on the business

– Containment

–DR/BC/System recovery

–Manual/backup processes

–Tolerance/co-existence w/malware

• If current efforts unsuccessful – what should we do

• Do we need to notify anybody

Incident Commander's Guidance

• Are we on the right track?

• What information do we need to know and don't currently have?

• What additional tasks need to be assigned?

• Expectations by the next status brief

• Contact the Incident Commander/Task Force ASAP if any of the following occur:

Next Status Brief

• When

• Where

• Send slide input at least 15 minutes prior to Joe.Shmoe@XYZ.com

• These slides can be accessed online at: <your intranet site here>

I have a couple of comments regarding this status brief. Assumption management is critical in a crisis when you do not have all the information that you need. This is especially true with a zero-day outbreak. The second issue becomes one of "slide management." Anybody who has served on a military staff has seen the effort necessary to manage getting all the slides in on time, last minute updates, and so on. The payoff is when you have everyone's attention and you can quickly roll through the presentation, the entire team is getting the update, and the decision-maker is prepared to make decisions.

This completes this chapter on the Malware CIRP execution. The next chapter will discuss the termination, post incident tasks, and maintaining your Malware CIRP.

Your Malware Outbreak CIRP: Post Incident Planning and Maintenance

We are finally at the last section of the Malware CIRP. You learned previously about preparing for crisis and the execution of the CIRP during time of actual crisis. This section of the plan covers four main areas:

▶ Determining when an incident is really over

▶ Maintaining the currency of your plan

▶ Learning from executing and testing your plan (Lessons Learned)

▶ Testing your plan

Ultimately, your crisis will come to pass. It's a good idea to document what criteria needs to be met in order for an incident to be terminated. This helps you in a couple of ways. As you progress through your incident, you have an idea of the criteria that will be used to terminate the incident. If you are the incident coordinator, this is something you should start tracking as you see things winding down. Secondly, often after an incident, folks are basically in a hurry to wrap things up and move on. This is another point of friction. You also risk losing resources toward the end of your incident because folks may feel things are done and they have day jobs to go back to. Having a pre-agreed definition of success helps you hold the response together until it your crisis is truly resolved. This is also something you put together with your advisory committee when you build your plan. Listed next is what I have in the CIRP.

Incident Termination

Prior to terminating a data breach response, it is critical to ensure that all due diligence has been performed. The termination phase of a data breach is a critical time to ensure that all the necessary actions have been performed, that all requirements for evidence retention have been identified, and that a mutually agreed upon standard has been met in resolving the computer data breach.

Criteria for Terminating an Incident

The criteria for terminating an incident are listed as follows:

i. Was the source of the malware identified, contained, and eradicated?

ii. Did we confirm that other XYZ systems were not affected?

   iii. Are there any significant activities outstanding that require the immediate attention of the Malware Outbreak task force to resolve?

   iv. What systems and/or processes failed to prevent, detect, and/or correct the breach of the affected system?

   v. Have the appropriate changes been made to prevent future outbreaks of this malware from affecting XYZ systems?

   vi. Has a discussion with members of the Malware Outbreak task force occurred, and was there consensus that the malware outbreak has been resolved?

Premature termination of an incident can expose the corporation to unnecessary risk.

Decision Process for Terminating an Incident

The formal process for terminating an incident is as follows:

▶ Based on the Incident Termination criteria listed above,

▶ With recommendations provided by the following members of the task force:

Group	POC
CISO	Suzy Queue
Data Center Operations	Brad Jones
Customer Services	Steve Jones
Service and Support	David Jones
ISOC	Neal Jones

▶ The Incident Commander will ultimately make the decision to officially terminate the incident based on the recommendations presented to them by the members of the task force listed above.

This last section of the CIRP is the smallest but seems to take the largest amount of individual and organizational commitment. The constant maintenance and improvement of a plan are difficult tasks to accomplish. All too often, plans are written and placed on a shelf, only to be forgotten. Unfortunately, with a malware plan there is no compliance box to be checked, and it is really difficult to get resources to maintain the plan when you can't waive the compliance flag to rally resources. Over time, as the organization changes and requirements change, the plan becomes outdated, only to be irrelevant when it is needed later. One of the most important concepts that need to be conveyed is that your plan is a living document and requires constant attention. We're going to discuss this topic in greater detail, but first here is what is recorded in the actual CIRP.

Plan Maintenance

Overview

This plan is only valuable as long as it is relevant. The objective of maintaining a plan is to ensure that at time of immediate execution, the plan provides relevant information to ensure successful execution. To this end, it is incumbent upon all those who will be potentially called to respond to a malware outbreak to ensure their information within the plan is current and relevant.

Quarterly Updates

Verification/Updates of Perishable Data

The ISOC is responsible for verifying the currency of all components of this plan to ensure that the information necessary for the execution of this plan is current. Upgrade information will be listed in the "Updating and Synchronization" table in the "Plan Structure" section listed previously in the "Plan Introduction" portion of the plan.

Incorporation of Previous Lessons Learned

Lessons Learned input should be tracked by the ISOC for inclusion into subsequent versions of the computer incident response plan.

Prior to including any recommendation made in a Lessons Learned, it is imperative that the recommendation be socialized to all participants of the plan for their approval.

Lesson Learned recommendations should be e-mailed to the primary participants (those defined as "involved" in the Major Mobilization matrix) for their input. The CISO has final approval authority for implementing a Lessons Learned recommendation. The manager of the ISOC is responsible for accepting, tracking, routing, coordinating the decision-making process, and including successful recommendations into the updated version of the data breach incident response plan.

Annual Testing of the Plan

Requirement

Industry best practices require that all incident response plans be "tested" on an annual basis. Plan validation typically requires the involvement of all anticipated participants to ensure that if the plan were to be executed, it would have current information, work within the current structure and staffing of XYZ, and be immediately executable as written.

Exercise Mechanics

There are a number of ways to exercise an incident response plan. The U.S. military spends millions of dollars testing contingency plans for potential crises around the globe. These very complex exercises involve persons who would be expected to execute the plan, simulated potential adversaries, control persons simulating external entities that would influence the execution of the plan, and evaluators of the performance of personnel executing the plan. These large-scale exercises evaluate both the plan and the persons anticipated to execute the plan.

The objective within XYZ is to evaluate the plan and not the participants. The annual test should focus on the following objectives:

1. Is the information in the plan current and relevant?
2. Are the processes listed within the plan effective within the current XYZ environment?
3. Are the proper persons involved in the execution of the plan?
4. Are the processes listed in the plan current with the industry standard best practices?
5. Have we exposed the plan to all potentially involved parties from both within XYZ and outside partners/participants for their validation?

The exercise of the computer incident response plan will involve the following steps:

1. Notify and assemble all potentially involved parties per the incident response plan.
2. Have participants review the current plan.
3. Provide them with a scenario describing a potential malware outbreak.
4. Have the participants of the plan "talk through" what their roles and responsibilities would be according to the plan and based on the scenario.

5. Be sure to stick to a reasonable timeline and sequence of events.

6. Focus on those tasks that require coordination with other entities both inside of XYZ and outside.

7. Attempt to conduct at least one status report and decision briefing.

8. Provide opportunities for all members to discuss their actions and identify issues/improvements.

9. Consider realistic "what if" situations which involve assumptions regarding the availability of resources (i.e., "We'd call Mike") or the behavior of outside parties (i.e., the FBI would never show up prior to this step), and see if the plan is overly dependent on certain assumptions or resources.

Record(s) Retention

All records pertaining to the maintenance of the incident response plan should be retained by XYZ. In the event it becomes necessary to demonstrate XYZ's commitment to performing the necessary due diligence, information regarding all Lessons Learned inputs, and annual test documentation shall be maintained by the ISOC and available for inspection.

The section above is listed in the actual plan. This is very similar (if not copied) from the Data Breach CIRP. The challenge with testing the malware plan is twofold: you not only don't have the compliance "hammer," but most of the technical resources you need are already buried in regular day-to-day work. Lately I have been leveraging any execution of the plan within the last 12 months as an "annual test." This is cheating, maybe, but it's really about taking a point in time and evaluating the relevancy of the plan during the few opportunities when you can get all the players together and focused on a malware scenario (even if it is a real one). You still should be validating your references; your Point of Contact listing should be checked every quarter, and so on.

It's kind of a shame. I personally believe we are going to have to take this task more seriously in the near future. Jeff Klaben mentioned at the beginning of this book the "Here you have" e-mail virus that was attributed to "the Iraqi Resistance." This was a very poor beginning of what I think will become the IEDs" of the Internet. Malware response efforts will need to become more important, because these cyber-based terrorist attacks will become increasingly deliberate and destructive.

Closing Thoughts

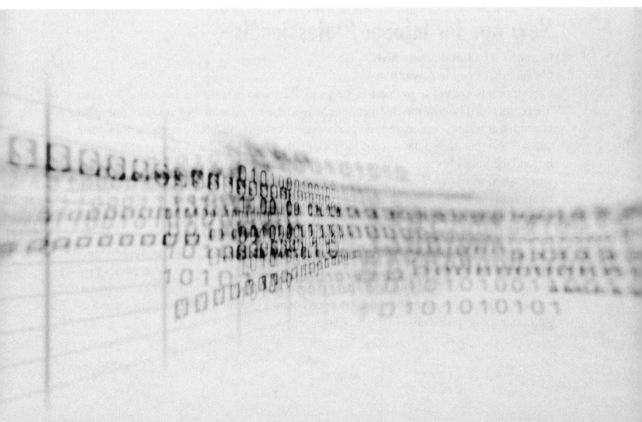

I t is my sincere hope that you found this book to be worth the money you spent on it. Actually, I hope you found this book to be worth far more than the money you spent on it. (Do you know how much one of the big consulting firms would charge to write a CIRP for you?) If all you do is take the different sections of the executable CIRPs from the book, do some cut and pastes, global replace all functions, and make this your own plan, you're probably better off than the majority of companies out there. Unfortunately, however, just having a plan isn't sufficient anymore.

When I was originally approached to write this book for McGraw-Hill, I was reluctant. I already had plenty to do, and the effort and time needed to write a book seemed to be too much. But as I started to dwell on this for awhile, I felt an obligation to write this book. I am growing increasingly concerned that as a profession, and for that matter as a nation, we are still in an old, outdated paradigm when it comes to computer security—naïve to a world around us that has changed so much, so incredibly fast, right in front of our very eyes. We are blissfully unaware of what's really going on in the Cyber-domain.

I would like to spend the next several pages discussing why I think we need newer/better paradigms as information security professionals, and maybe even as a nation.

New Age for InfoSec Professionals

In fourteen hundred ninety-two
Columbus sailed the ocean blue.

I was trying to convey to my non-IT savvy mother, who is somewhere around 70 years of age, this idea of how the Internet has changed the world and what is really going on beneath our noses. I compared today's world to what it must have been back in 1492, when Columbus sailed the seas of blue. Back then, the world was flat. If you went beyond the visual horizon, you would fall off the planet. Our knowledge of the oceans was limited to what we could see and sometimes touch. There were sea-monsters out there, ready to kill anyone who dared challenge the known universe. The vast resources of the planet were largely unknown to the civilized masses and waiting to be seized by those who dared to try.

Today, many of us look at the Internet much like folks in 1492 looked at the horizon. Very few of us realize the vast opportunity for exploitation that lies out there. Most of us are ignorant of these technologies that we depend on, and the Internet has become a repeat of history in which the more advanced people exploit the opportunities that lie in abundance at the expense of the less advanced.

Today, identity theft impacts 15 million Americans at a cost of $50 billion. Botnets own several *million* PCs. China was able to hack into Google (which employs some of the brightest minds in Silicon Valley) and steal its "Secret Sauce." Microsoft has so many vulnerabilities that the second Tuesday of every month they provide a *list* of them to the world. Small- and medium-sized organizations are being destroyed by financial account takeover attacks that rob them of all their cash. There is nothing like coming into your office on Monday only to find out all the money you need to pay employees and suppliers is *gone*.

Most of us are completely unaware of what lies beyond the horizon, or the battles being fought under the seas. We are only now becoming more aware of how all this continues to impact our world. I believe we need to address five fundamental paradigms within the field of information security if we are ever going to make gains against these extremely competent adversaries.

Paradigm #1: The New Consciousness of the Zero-Day Attack

It used to be in the "good ol' days," back when InfoSec mostly worried about those 15-year-old hackers who were out there making fun of us corporate stiffs, someone would find a new vulnerability, report it to the world, and the race was on. Once the new vulnerability was announced, parallel efforts would begin either to exploit or mitigate the vulnerability. I guess you could call the day the vulnerability was made known to the world "D-Day," to leverage military parlance. The good guys raced to repair (patch) this new vulnerability against the bad guys who would race to engineer an exploit leveraging that vulnerability. The winners usually were the ones who got to the unsuspecting computer first.

Then something happened to make the life of an InfoSec person even more interesting. New attacks out there leveraged a new vulnerability, but the vulnerability hadn't been publicly disclosed or gone through the race discussed in the previous paragraph. This was a "pre-D-Day" attack, or what the industry started calling the *zero-day attack*.

Zero-day attacks are the worst kind, because the industry doesn't know about them and doesn't have time to address the vulnerability. Back in the "age of innocence," zero-days were the worst-case scenario. These were the *uber* hacks. The prevailing due diligence was to keep up on your patching process and keep all your security tools current with the latest signatures to identify potential attacks. The focus of the industry was winning the race to address the known vulnerability. And although many were sounding the alarm, the zero-day attack was the "elephant in the corner" that most hoped would spare their organization for an easier target.

Today things are different—sort of. Don't get me wrong. Patching known vulnerabilities is still *very* important. The lack of patching makes it much easier for the bad guys and much more likely that your organization will be attacked. Besides, there are plenty of folks out there taking on easy targets with tools available on the Internet.

But today we need a different mentality on zero-days. Well, actually, this mentality has been around the Washington Beltway for a very long time. Today a good zero-day exploit can be the keys to the kingdom—that is, the true zero-day that is engineered in secret, known to just a very, very few and in the possession of those who are willing and able to do bad things with your information. This zero-day has tremendous value, depending on what it is able to do to the targeted system.

Imagine for a minute that you found the key (I think they used to call them skeleton keys) that would open any front door in your neighborhood. The angel on your shoulder is telling you to turn it in to the police. Or maybe let the lock makers know their locks are no longer valid. But the devil on your other shoulder is telling you this key is very valuable. You can use it. Maybe you should make some copies and sell it to a few folks. Maybe you're really good at finding these types of keys and you should develop a service that helps people find/make these keys. Maybe you just want to look around the inside of your obnoxious neighbor's home. The point is that everyone has the expectation that their locks work. They don't know there is a master key out there. They certainly don't know that you have the master key. Most will never doubt that their locks work. You are free to come and go as long as you're careful not to be seen or heard.

An ever-increasing group of folks have exploited this new consciousness. While the rest of us are chasing down known vulnerabilities and thinking we're "safe" because we're current with all the known threats, somebody, somewhere has figured out that there is money to be made if you can develop zero-day exploits and keep them secret. Companies such as iDefense, Accuvant, and ManTech (just to name a very few) all sell their wares to three-letter agencies within the Beltway (and who else?) developing zero-day exploits.

Don't think for a minute that organized crime, making millions in stolen credit card numbers and other attacks, wouldn't set aside a few bucks to come up with their own zero-day exploits or that some nation-state interested in your "secret sauce" (such as Aurora) wouldn't have their legions of cyber-warriors pointed at you. Many of these efforts don't require the skills of an under-employed and thoroughly frustrated PhD quality scientist, say, in a place like the former Soviet Union to work. For you see, a zero-day is really a vulnerability that is not known to the various appliances into which so many within InfoSec have placed such a considerable amount of money/effort/trust. If you can make a known vulnerability unknown to these common appliances, you have a poor man's zero-day. The manufacturers of these off-the-shelf InfoSec appliances don't check to see who are the good guys or the bad guys. Criminals today can easily buy these devices (better yet, with a stolen credit card number) and install them in their offices/garages/labs and simply test them until they find out what works.

Tipping point—one of the leading intrusion prevention and detection (appliance) companies has its own "Zero-day Initiative" (www.ZeroDayInitiative.com): they *pay you* for your zero-day discoveries. What a great idea, unless of course you work for an Internet security research company in some *fill-in-the-blank-istan* country and all your discoveries go off to a different department. The company has millions of dollars and pays your salary on a regular basis, so it must be legitimate, right?

Pacific Gas & Electric, the utility company for the San Francisco Bay Area, recently hired a retired CIA-type to be their director of information security intelligence—a smart move, from my point of view. He presented at a Secret Service Electronic Crime Task Force (ECTF) meeting that the going price for a zero-day exploit on the Internet was in the neighborhood of $50K. Do you know how much money Osama bin Laden spent training people to fly the airplanes on 9/11? Considerably more than that.

A very glaring example of leveraging zero-days is the Stuxnet virus, which had (depending on what media source you want to believe) four zero-day exploits within it. Although some have deduced this was created by a *nation-state* player, the concept is the same. Amateurs wait for the next vulnerability. Professionals find/make their own. Now some of you reading this may think that since Stuxnet was a very specific virus, that happened to be most effective against Iranian nuclear processing facilities, that this doesn't apply to you. Well not so fast. This new consciousness extends to all technologies and is limited only by one's imagination and will.

One case was more of a physical hack involving credit card point of sale (POS) systems in western Canada a couple of years ago. When all was said and done, it was an organized crime group out of Malaysia that perpetrated this attack methodology into Canada, the United States, and Australia. What they did was to find a way to circumvent the tamper-proof capability of a very popular POS terminal so they could reengineer the internal components to capture and extract credit card data. When I first heard of this, I asked one of my folks to research the Internet for any information on this type of POS device. What we found was totally in keeping with this new zero-day mentality. Listed on a web site called Guru.com was a "Project request" for someone to develop engineering specifications to provide these exact devices with what they called "wireless back-up capability." In essence, they needed an electrical engineering–type of guru to help them design the hack. The posted price for the work was $5K. Now I'm not sure that this was the eventual route that was followed. But the main idea here is that people aren't waiting around for someone else to find and post to the world the next vulnerability. They're doing it themselves and keeping it to themselves.

The implications of this new mentality go beyond just the losses derived from the theft of credit card numbers. Matthew Todd detailed the payment card industry (PCI) and its efforts to secure credit card information. As a result of this $5K hack, an entire line of POS devices were "de-listed" by PCI. I was told that there were upwards of 500,000 of these devices in use in North America. Suddenly, these devices were no longer authorized for use. So the company that made them and spent countless dollars in R&D, production, and sales, and the various businesses that spent millions on installing these devices, were basically left out in the cold because someone had the vision and daring (and $5K) to challenge this technology. Now there's more to this story, and some of this has not been confirmed, but at a high level, this is what's going on in the world around us. This isn't an isolated incident. Fuel dispenser POS breaches are rampant. A Northern California grocery store chain, Lucky Stores, recently announced that more than 20 of it stores had their self-checkout POS systems breached, much in the same fashion as what happened two or three years ago.

My weekday mornings all start with talk radio. That's what my wife has the alarm clock set to. I usually don't pay much attention to it, but one morning the hosts were talking about some new TSA (Transportation Security Administration) measures that went into affect that day and it caught my attention. Actually the new measures didn't catch my attention; it was the spontaneous comment that one of the hosts made that caught my attention. Now this isn't verbatim, but it was something like this: "You know, Bill [whoever the other talking head was], it just kills me. Just when we're getting used to the old [TSA] measures, they go and change things. I just don't understand why we have to keep going through all these changes."

I was dumbfounded. I wanted to call in and tell her that you're going through all these changes because there are people out there who want to kill Americans. Every time the TSA comes up with a method to protect you, the bad people find a way to get around it. This is the nature of conflict. This is the essence of security: that for every measure you put out there to protect something, bad people develop a counter measure.

It dawned on me that this is probably the same way of thinking for many in InfoSec. There are too many InfoSec professionals out there who believe they can simply buy the latest firewall intrusion prevention/detection system—whatever box you want—install it, power it up, and they are good to go. This sounds obvious enough, but there are too many folks who fall for what I call this "Green Light Syndrome." For too many, InfoSec is an "engineering" effort and not a "security" effort. So when these devices get bypassed, they are surprised. I was recently listening to the former CISO of one of the nation's major healthcare organizations basically tell the audience that he felt one of the major failures of InfoSec was that the majority of vendors failed to deliver on the promise of their technologies. I couldn't help wonder if he was one of those "Green Light" folks who also complains about all the TSA changes.

The military has a very different view when trying to deter a committed adversary. There is a basic rule of thumb that for every obstacle you put in place, if you intend for it to be effective, you need to be able to observe when your adversary attempts to breach it and have a "plan B" to deal with their efforts. So when you put out that minefield, you have a team of soldiers observe it, and when the bad guys try to breach it, you shoot/shell them—something like that. The military just assumes that when they place an obstacle in front of a determined enemy, the enemy will attempt to breach it as part of their effort to achieve their objective(s).

Many in the InfoSec community speak of "defense in depth." And for too many, that simply means adding more of the same boxes throughout the enterprise. Now there may be good reason for that type of deployment, or that's what the salesperson told you to do with the product, but I think at a minimum we need to start rethinking defense in depth to be more of the military model. We need to start challenging this mentality. Now don't get me wrong. I'm not telling you that these technologies don't work. They do work. Bazillions of attacks every day are very successfully prevented/detected by these technologies. That's not the point. Far too many in this profession are lulled into confidence because these technologies are so successful at preventing *known* attacks.

More of us should be kept awake at night by the knowledge that there are very capable people out there who know how to get around these devices. And these people are willing and able to breach your organization quietly, patiently, professionally, and at great consequence to your organization should you fall in their crosshairs. Good incident response planning is just one of the tools at your disposal to deal with this new paradigm. The knowledge you garnered from this book should help you prepare for this eventuality.

Paradigm #2: The Need for Transparent Due Diligence

I think we need to rethink this idea of due diligence for InfoSec professionals. The challenges faced by CISOs/CSOs today are only going to get more difficult. Matthew Todd did a wonderful job detailing the majority of the numerous laws, guidelines, frameworks, and so on, out there. We can choose to leverage these, or, as is the case for many of us, we are obligated to comply with some. As the cyber-threat continues to grow, legislation might be the only practical mechanism to force organizations to spend money that often (but not always) doesn't help their bottom line to enforce a mechanism of industry standard due diligence.

The problem I have is that today what we have is a patchwork of various requirements for various types of information. Remember that I've come from a military background where everything is based on the construct that *requirements* drive *execution*, and you need to constantly *validate* that *execution* is actually supporting *requirements*. This *requirements/execution/validation* loop is the basis for how things get done.

In order for this construct to work, you have to be able to understand your requirements. When you have all these various requirements that Matthew talked about coming at you, and you still have to serve the primary requirements of the organization you support, things can get awfully confusing, especially when these requirements are based on specific types of information, such as Payment Card Industry (PCI), protected health information (PHI), or personally identifiable information (PII). Organizations currently working to combine all these various requirements into a common framework are finding it is not a trivial task.

I think we're going to need to look at something like the approach PCI has taken, but expand it beyond just credit card numbers/data. The idea is you take an industry best practice framework (e.g., ISO27K) and apply it to the information you should be protecting. Establish a process of validation to ensure what you're actually accomplishing (executing) is meeting the requirements you've identified. Then finally, have this audited by someone from outside the organization with some knowledge of these things. Now I'm not suggesting that you follow all of the PCI implementation. For example, PCI mandates that you encrypt all credit card data. I'm not suggesting that you encrypt all the data you deem sensitive. What I am suggesting is that you develop and mature a process through which you "ask the question," based on the framework, to determine what approach makes the most sense based on your circumstances.

Ultimately, the InfoSec organization will have limited funds and resources to devote and tough decisions will need to be made (more on that in the next paradigm). This effort needs to be transparent within the leadership of the organization. This approach should push the organization to define a broader scope of the information assets that would be of interest to criminals and competitors, and not just the compliance folks. Hopefully, this will foster a more realistic understanding of what measures are available to protect these organizational assets.

I think there have been too many InfoSec leaders who have gotten by with the "trust me—I know what I'm doing" approach. The day will be upon us in the not-so-distant future where InfoSec professionals will have to be able to demonstrate quantifiable due diligence against an industry best practice framework that is validated by someone outside of the InfoSec organization. Good incident response planning is a helpful mechanism in demonstrating your due diligence and is typically required by most of the accepted industry frameworks/standards.

Paradigm #3: Consequence-Based Information Security

This third topic should not come as a surprise if you've read this book. This concept of consequence is key to both CIRPs and especially to the Malware Outbreak plan. Too many InfoSec professionals and vendors are solely focused on vulnerability and threat and ignore this concept of consequence. As I mentioned in Chapter 8, if you subscribe to the Department of Homeland Security's definition of risk, then you are aware that risk is defined as a vulnerability that is exploited by a threat that manifests some consequence(s) to the organization at large.

It's been said that if all you know how to use is a hammer, then every problem will be solved with a hammer. I think the same is true of this paradigm. The vast majority of InfoSec people are technical. They understand and probably are very fascinated with the vulnerability and threat aspect of InfoSec. They typically don't understand business or how the organization they support works. As a result, they usually don't comprehend how information risk manifests within their organization. They are unable to articulate their efforts in terms of *business consequence*. The effective CISOs/CSOs understand this and are often more successful in getting funds and organizational buy-in because they can speak of the business benefit (consequence).

This is more than just talking the talk with your business partners. InfoSec organizations typically have to struggle to get sufficient resources to battle the ever-increasing cyber-threat and to meet the wide range of contractual and statutory requirements that are out there. With these limited resources, InfoSec leadership needs to prioritize its efforts to ensure maximum effectiveness. All too often, the consequence of failing an audit is the only consequence-based decision most InfoSec professionals make.

As more organizations start to formalize their Enterprise Risk Management (ERM) efforts, organizations are becoming more risk aware and more conversant in the concept of risk management. But since most business (non-InfoSec) ERM is based on consequences and presented in business terms, InfoSec professionals risk having their concerns minimized because their relevance to the business cannot be adequately articulated. Their language is that of technical vulnerability and threat, and not of business consequence.

I guess it's been a couple of years now, but the U.S. Chamber of Commerce and a lot of other organizations came out with warnings about these "account takeover attacks" that were happening across the United States. Phishing e-mails would download browser-in-the-middle attacks onto the unsuspecting PC. So when (mostly small- and medium-sized) businesses, school districts, investors, or anybody who needed to go online and manage sizable sums of money, would log into their bank accounts, the bad guys were right there with them. Unfortunately, many of these victims would come in on a Monday morning only to find that all of their cash was gone from their bank accounts—typically transferred to an Eastern European bank outside of the reach of U.S. law enforcement.

For a small- to medium-sized business, the consequence of having all of your liquid capital stolen from you is a *business extinction* event (and unfortunately has been for many companies). The Fortune 100 company I was working with didn't think this type of attack would cause the business to fail, but there were eight-figure amounts at risk on any given day, and this was real money getting stolen. Only a couple of computers were used to transfer these funds by a small group of employees.

A threat and vulnerability approach would have treated these computers no differently than the other 50,000 computers that were in the company. But since we were aware of the *consequence* of this type of attack on this small group of PCs, we partnered with the Cash Management group and developed a full range of InfoSec and non-IT measures to counter this threat.

This is just an example of all those consequence-based concerns that InfoSec should be dealing with. And while the InfoSec masses are looking at firewalls, IPS/IDS, anti-virus measures, or trying to patch every one of the bazillion printers in the environment, who's looking out for cash management, board of director meeting minutes, merger and acquisition plans, executive compensation files, or anything else that's critical to protecting your organization from competitors and criminals? If you work in a company where its intellectual property *is* the business, you had better be focusing on the consequence of losing your IP and making sure your effort to mitigate that risk is your number one priority.

During the first Gulf War, a Marine Expeditionary Brigade afloat off the Kuwaiti coast caused the Iraqi army to have to spread a considerable share of its forces along the Kuwaiti coastline to prevent an amphibious attack. By expanding the attack surface that Saddam Hussein had to defend, it caused him to spread his forces out and weakened his ability to defend against the U.S. main attack from the south. Similarly, InfoSec professionals have way too much attack surface to defend. As criminal threats become even more lethal, successful organizations are going to have to concentrate their efforts around those areas of greatest consequence to the organization they support in order to be successful. We're also going to have to get comfortable with this concept of *intrusion tolerance*. I first heard of this at a US CERT GFIRST conference in 2006. The idea is the bad guys are already "inside the wire"—inside your enterprise. The main premise of intrusion tolerance is that you don't spend your time and efforts worrying about the small stuff. Focus on those assets that are most consequential to your organization ("Center of Gravity") and get to that other stuff when you can. This is a difficult concept for many to embrace but is absolutely necessary looking forward.

One other thing on consequence-based InfoSec: we need to get over this idea that we can prevent all bad things from happening. With limited resources defending an ever-expanding attack surface, we may be more practical if we take these low probability–high impact (consequence) events and use the necessary precautions to minimize the high impact part of the equation. By focusing on the consequence of the event, we can lower the overall risk. Cyber-insurance is an example of how you can mitigate the consequence of a low probability–high impact event. A good CIRP will also help you minimize the consequence (impact) of an incident.

Paradigm #4: The Constant Challenge of Change

Change is constant. I've always believed that. What's killing me these days is the *rate* of change. Social media is facilitating the toppling of governments in the Middle East. IT is dramatically changing the ways businesses interact with their customers. I was at a recent InfoSec seminar and heard from one of presenters that organized crime is now making more money from credit card theft than from the drug trade. Change is coming at us from all directions, and it makes me wonder if our current efforts will ever be sufficient.

In the time this book was being produced, the following occurred:

► VISA issued new guidance for credit card breaches.

► California passed new Data Breach notification legislation (SB-24).

► The Security and Exchange Commission (SEC) issued public guidance about credit card/data breach notification.

► The Ninth Circuit Court lowered the standing necessary to file a data breach claim (making it easier to get sued).

► A federal appeals court ruled in favor of the Hannaford (credit card breach) victims' damages for "preventative" measures (for example, credit monitoring) versus actual fraud losses.

All of these are important to the development of a data breach CIRP but unfortunately are not included in this book. The time it took to write/review/approve this book was outpaced by the speed and volume of change.

InfoSec professionals need to *expect* that today's efforts are temporary and that numerous forces out there will bring change to your doorstep. Whether it is the technology you deploy, the processes you follow, the laws you need to comply with, or the plans you produce, *everything* will be subject to the forces of change. InfoSec professionals must maintain a constant vigilance for the uncertainty of change and embrace the understanding that today's solution will rarely solve tomorrows challenge. Expect to respond to a new crisis.

I believe our ability to socialize among other professionals is a critical tool in addressing change. I'm particular to the InfraGard program that the FBI has sponsored across the nation, but any effort is beneficial. There are numerous organizations out there—the Information Systems Security Association (ISSA), Information Systems Audit and Control Association (ISACA), the Forum for Incident Response and Security Teams (FIRST), and the list goes on. These professional contacts are more than just a means for networking for that next job. These are key opportunities to learn from your peers what challenges they face and how they are addressing them. Most importantly, the ability to exchange timely and relevant information among security professionals is absolutely critical in this new age.

I'd like to provide a real-world case in which these types of relationships can be so helpful. I guess the first place to start is that this book is largely the result of my participation in the InfraGard program. It was my presentation with Jeff Klaben on Incident Response Planning at a quarterly InfraGard meeting that caught the eye of Amy Jollymore, an acquisitions editor for McGraw-Hill, who was in the audience.

Everybody who has contributed to this book I know through the InfraGard chapter. Remember in Chapter 3 where we talked about the proactive use of your plans during periods of heightened risk? In that instance, we proactively mobilized our malware CIRP based on knowledge of this e-mail worm that was spreading around the globe—an e-mail worm we would learn afterward was one of the worst in a decade. That morning, one of the first e-mails that caught my eye was from Matthew Todd. Matthew is the CSO for a financial firm in Silicon Valley, the president of our local InfraGard chapter of which I was on the board of directors, and he also contributed to this book. It was Matthew's e-mail about the e-mail worm that first got me concerned. About two hours later, the U.S. Secret Service, through their local Electronic Crime Task Force (ECTF, which holds quarterly meetings in just about every major city), sent out a warning about the worm to its distribution list. This emboldened my view that we needed to proactively mobilize our resources. When we then went to our subscription threat service and saw their confirmation of the threat, it seemed pretty obvious to me that we weren't going to be "crying wolf" and that I had sufficient cause for alarm. I just can't say enough about these organizations and how they improve your ability not only to come and hear about the latest and greatest, but to develop relationships with others who share your profession and concerns.

Paradigm #5: While We're All Focusing on the Silicon-Based Systems, the Bad Guys Are Targeting the Carbon-Based Ones

I don't mean to keep bashing technology, but like I mentioned in Paradigm 1, the bad guys simply find a way around our counter measures. They have found a very effective target for bypassing our protective technologies: our end users.

A number of influences are making end users the most important priority for InfoSec:

- ▶ The proliferation of PDAs (personal digital assistants), iPad/phones, and the Bring Your Own Device (BYOD) movement happening in numerous organizations

- ▶ Phishing, pretexting, and social media attacks directly targeting end users

- ▶ Solicitation and bribery

- ▶ WikiLeaks, aka the "moral imperative" to set information free

I think we need to look at end users in a whole new light. This isn't just about doing a better job of awareness training, even though I think we need to start looking at awareness training differently than we do today, but more on that later. We need to understand that our end users are typically overwhelmed by other needs and not focused on InfoSec concerns. Most aren't even what I would consider IT-savvy. But it's more than that. I believe InfoSec has worked its way in most organizations into an adversarial role with those who conduct the "business" of your business. And as such, end users will rarely reach out to InfoSec for help on those questionable calls.

Let me give you an example. A company I consult with detected an outbound e-mail to an AOL account with a spreadsheet that contained the PII (Social Security number, date of birth, and so on) of around 15,000 employees. Since this was a serious violation of policy, their ISOC red lights went off. What I would come to find out was an amazing story of an employee's commitment to her family *and* her job. The lady in question did not have a laptop to take home. She did everything on a PC at her desk. The quarter-end report was due for some sort of regulatory requirement (I didn't get into the details) and had to get done. This woman's husband had just gone through cancer surgery, and they weren't sure he was going to live through the recuperation at home. This woman's first response was that she was taking time off to take care of her husband for what might have been the last days of his life. But she agreed to work on the report from home while he was sleeping, knowing there were serious consequences for the company should it not be filed on time (she was the only who could do it). These folks all read the privacy policy. They were all aware of the rules. It dawned on me that although they knew the policies, they didn't know who to call for advice, or they feared they would be given a hard-line answer. "It's better to ask forgiveness than permission" had been their approach when dealing with InfoSec.

There's another way bad people (or maybe "wrong" people is a more correct term) are getting sensitive information from your end users: they're asking them for it, and sometimes even paying them. Companies out there such as Global Primary Research and Tribeca Insights are reaching out to your end users/employees. Global Primary Research got in trouble with the SEC because the information they were getting from folks was later used by investors and considered inside information. Several folks were actually convicted in federal court for providing that information. Now the SEC cared because the information gained was considered insider trading. Do you think the SEC would care if it was your company's "secret sauce" or perhaps your marketing strategy? How about quarterly sales results? Don't think for a minute folks won't just call and ask, or in the case of some of these research firms, pay an employee $200 an hour for being an "expert consultant."

Phishing is starting to become a regular problem, and I think too many are thinking the latest technology will solve it. A friend of mine was telling me about an instance at his company in which a Bank of America (phishing) e-mail was sent to all the three-letter vice presidents listed on their annual report. Of course, it got by the e-mail filter and ended up in these folks' inboxes. I had helped them write a phishing protocol, so they immediately enacted that. After following the protocol, they found out that three folks had clicked the link. This next part will simply amaze you. Two of the VPs suspected the e-mail was suspicious, so they had their executive admins (EAs) click the link. The third called the local IT field services guy—so what did he do? He opened it on his laptop and clicked the link. I'm not making this stuff up. (Talk about taking one for the team.) Fortunately, in this instance, the outbound web proxy blocked the malicious URL (this doesn't always happen), so they didn't have to go through the whole decontamination process and figure out what/if information was stolen.

I'm going to end this discussion with the topic of *awareness training*. I think we need to get beyond the typical awareness training. You know what I am talking about. This is the annual privacy training where you skip over all the content and just answer the questions so you can get back to your real business at hand. It's that flyer that comes with your paystub once a year that promptly gets discarded.

We need to start looking at awareness as part of our InfoSec arsenal. Start by addressing the various high-risk audiences in your environment. You should probably determine what information in your organization is at risk—and not just compliance risk (such as SOX and PCI). I'm talking about information that would also benefit your competitors and criminals. Start with the folks who handle that sensitive data. Everyone in HR and labor relations would be on this list for all the PII they handle. Workers' comp handles PII and PHI. I mentioned cash management earlier in the chapter. Every organization at some point has to pay its bills. The people who manage your money are an example of a high-risk group. Another type of group has to do with technical nuances. Some examples of these groups: iPad/iPhone users who are on your network (or any other BYOD); folks who are authorized to use social media at work (assuming you limit that kind of thing); people with admin rights on their PCs; and the list goes on. All these different audiences are end users who need to be aware of the value of the information they are supposed to be protecting and the threats that are out there targeting them. I think we need to go that one step further than simply signing them up for some customized InfoSec awareness training. I think we need to take things to the next level and actually make an effort to "engage" with these groups as much as possible. Meet with them; sit through one of their team meetings. See their world from their view and be prepared to take opportunities for improvement to InfoSec and IT. Hopefully, you should develop a working relationship with these users so that they realize that InfoSec is there to support them when they have that questionable call to make. Maybe even develop an ongoing dialog so that when new threats emerge, or their requirements change, each of you is comfortable calling the other. So when that difficult situation comes up, they will reach out to you for help instead of defaulting to asking for forgiveness later. Our end user communities are a major vulnerability and they are being targeted, and we need to do more.

Thank you for taking the time to read this book. Thank you for letting me get on my soap box. Again, I sincerely hope you found reading this book to be worth your time.

—N. K. McCarthy

Appendixes

Useful Online Resources

L isted here are links you may find of interest as an information security professional:

- ▶ **VISA issued new guidance for credit card breaches**
  http://usa.visa.com/download/merchants/cisp_what_to_do_if_compromised.pdf

- ▶ **California passed new legislation (SB-24)**
  http://www.leginfo.ca.gov/pub/11-12/bill/sen/sb_0001-0050/sb_24_bill_20110
  819_enrolled.pdf

- ▶ **The Security and Exchange Commission (SEC) issued public guidance about credit card/data breach notification**
  http://www.sec.gov/divisions/corpfin/guidance/cfguidance-topic2.htm

- ▶ **The Ninth Circuit Court lowered the standing necessary to file a data breach claim (making it easier to get sued)**
  http://www.lexology.com/library/detail.aspx?g=06c13e43-ed9a-4173-b522-25d
  1ef124f20

- ▶ **A Federal Appeals Court ruled in favor of the Hannaford (credit card breach) victims' damages for "preventative" measures (for example, credit monitoring) versus actual fraud losses**
  http://www.infolawgroup.com/2011/10/articles/damages/federal-appeals-court-
  holds-identity-theft-insurancecredit-monitoring-costs-constitute-damages-in-
  hannaford-breach-case/

- ▶ **Infragard information**
  http://www.infragard.net/

- ▶ **ISSA information**
  http://ISSA.org

- ▶ **ISACA information**
  http://www.ISACA.org

- ▶ **FIRST information**
  http://www.first.org/

- ▶ **US CERT GFIRST information**
  http://www.us-cert.gov/GFIRST/

▶ **U.S. Secret Service Electronic Crimes Task Force (ECTF) information**
http://www.secretservice.gov/ectf.shtml

▶ **PCI DSS**
https://www.pcisecuritystandards.org/security_standards/documents.php?
document=pci_dss_v2-0#pci_dss_v2-0

▶ **HITECH**
http://www.hhs.gov/ocr/privacy/hipaa/understanding/coveredentities/breachnoti
ficationifr.html

Computer Incident Response Plan (CIRP) Management Checklist

T he purpose of this checklist is to provide an initial technology-agnostic assessment of a potential system compromise. Completion of this document is required prior to briefing senior management during an incident response.

❑ **Unusual activity in the access or system logs**
[Detail the type of activity, when noticed, and what makes it different from usual activity.]

❑ **Recent changes to the system**
[Detail any recent changes to the system that are within the relevant timeframe of the suspected incident. Be sure to highlight any changes that appear to be suspect.]

❑ **New user or super user IDs created**
[Identify any user IDs that were created during the timeframe of the suspected incident. Highlight any IDs that appear to be suspect.]

❑ **Deleted log files**
[Identify any log files that have been deleted during the timeframe of the suspected incident. Highlight any log deletions that appear to be suspect.]

❑ **Deleted or altered system files**
[Identify any system files that have been deleted or altered during the timeframe of the suspected incident. Highlight any of these files that appear to be suspect.]

❑ **Recent super user activity**
[Identify any super user activity during the timeframe of the suspected incident. Highlight any activity that appears to be suspect.]

❑ **Recent escalation of privileges**
[Identify any escalation of privileges during the timeframe of the suspected incident. Highlight any activity that appears to be suspect.]

❑ **Recent off-hour activity**
[Identify any off-hour activity during the timeframe of the suspected incident. Highlight any activity that appears to be suspect.]

❑ **Recent file transfers from the system**
[Identify any file transfers from the system during the timeframe of the suspected incident. Highlight any transfers that appear to be suspect.]

❑ **Business impact**
[Identify any changes to the normal processes/uses of the suspected system by the end user/business user during the timeframe of the suspected incident. Highlight any changes or activities that appear to be suspect.]

Glossary

account takeover attacks   Targeting the financial transactions of organizations, cyber-criminals (*see* APT) attempt to break into online banking transactions to steal funds by gaining access to online accounts and transferring funds to offshore accounts. These attacks have been successful against small- and medium-sized organizations with losses in the six- to seven-figure range. The U.S. Chamber of Commerce, NACHA, the Electronic Payments Association, FBI, and U.S. Secret Service have issued advisories. The problem was so bad at one point the Financial Services-Information Sharing and Analysis Center (FS-ISAC) established an Account Takeover Attack Resource Center for use by victims.

acquiring banks   A Payment Card Industry (PCI) term referring to the financial institutions through which your organization processes its credit and debit transactions.

anti-virus (AV)   Similar to a medical vaccination, this computer technology protects your computer from known computer viruses/attacks.

APT   Advance persistent threat. A characterization of the new cyber-threat that is professional, patient, and covert, typically in the form of nation–state actors or organized crime. Unlike hackers in the past who sought notoriety, with this new threat, attackers seek to profit from their endeavors. Many have equated the skills and methods of today's APTs with those of "A-team" organizations such as the National Security Agency (NSA).

AUP   Acceptable use policies. Establishes expectations among users of what computer behavior is allowed by the organization providing the technology.

BRMs   Business relationship managers. In many large organizations, this role bridges the needs of the business users with the capabilities of the IT organization.

browser-in-the-middle   A type of attack methodology used in account takeover attacks (see preceding definition) in which a third party surreptitiously injects itself between the unsuspecting victim and the victim's online bank account. Once "in the middle," the criminal is able to observe and/or alter the interaction between the victim and the financial organization to steal funds from the account.

BYOD   Bring your own device. With the proliferation of handheld technology devices (such as PDAs), there is a growing demand on businesses from their senior leadership, employees, and customers to integrate these privately owned personal technologies into the infrastructure of the business.

CA SB-24   California's latest data breach notification law.

CFO   Chief financial officer. The corporate officer primarily responsible for handling the financial matters of the organization.

choke points   Taken from military jargon, choke points are locations within a geographical area that cause the concentration of forces into a small area to pass through some form of constriction, ultimately causing congestion. In the context of this book, choke points are network connections that tend to aggregate a large amount of traffic between significant entities in an organization or outside of the organization (via an Internet connection, for example). Network choke points play a significant role in the development of a containment strategy for use during a malware outbreak.

CIA   Central Intelligence Agency. The primary intelligence gathering organization for the United States.

CIO   Chief information officer. The corporate officer primarily responsible for handling the Information Technology matters of the organization.

CIRP   Computer Incident Response Plan. The manifestation of preparation for a cyber crisis.

CIRP SWAT   See CIRP. Special Weapons and Tactics (SWAT): much like the 2003 movie starring Samuel Jackson and Colin Farrell, the SWAT team is typically a group of the best cops that is charged with dealing with the most dangerous situations by utilizing, you guessed it, special weapons and tactics. In the context of this book, "SWAT" is used to describe computer professionals who have an exceptional knowledge of the various technologies that could be involved in a data breach. A term with similar meaning could be the Computer Emergency Response Team (CERT). We've also heard the term "*SMEs With AttiTudes.*"

CISO   Chief Information Security Officer. The person typically charged with the responsibility of protecting the sensitive information of an organization.

CISP   Cardholder Information Security Program. This Visa security program was the predecessor to PCI.

CMMI   Capability Maturity Model Integration. A methodology used to define and help to improve the maturity levels of processes.

COBIT   COBIT is a framework for IT governance and controls, established and maintained by ISACA (Information Systems Audit and Control Association).

consequence management   Based on the principle that *risk* is the combination of *vulnerability*, exploited by a *threat*, that manifests a *consequence* (impact) to an organization/entity, consequence management is the effort to minimize the impact of an event. In the context of this book, consequence management means focusing on minimizing the business/organizational impact as part of an overall response effort.

CPP   Common point of purchase. The dreaded phone call you get from the credit card companies or law enforcement that based on usage patterns of compromised cards, your organization appears to be the "one thing in common" or the "common point of purchase" that suggests the compromise originated from your organization.

CSO   Chief security officer. Unlike CISOs, CSOs tend to have a broader range of security responsibilities that may also include physical security, risk management, and so on. They are also usually higher up in the corporate reporting structure, which is often an indicator of the importance of their role to the organization.

CVV2   Card Verification Value (2nd edition). This is either the three-digit number on the back of your credit card, or the four-digit number on the front if you use an American Express card, which is often used to verify that you have the card in your presence.

DHS   Department of Homeland Security. The cabinet level organization within the U.S. government tasked with protecting the U.S. "homeland" from terrorist attacks, man-made and natural disasters.

DHS NIPP   *See* DHS. National Infrastructure Protection Plan. This is a gigantic plan (something like 10 inches thick if you stack it all together) that ties all the various efforts at the national level to protect the critical infrastructure of the United States. It includes a range of threat scenarios that include biological warfare, dirty bombs, and cyber-attacks.

DLP   Data Loss Prevention. A technology that "watches" what's leaving your organization and either blocks it or notifies you when sensitive information is leaving.

DNS   Domain Name Services. An Internet service that maps a URL to an actual Internet Protocol (IP) address. Think of it as an automatic 411 service, but for the Internet instead of your phone. You tell it, "I want to look at the Google web site (Google.com)," and DNS translates that request to an actual IP number (72.14.204.100).

DOJ   Department of Justice. The federal executive department of the U.S. government responsible for the enforcement of federal laws and the administration of justice.

DR   Disaster recovery. In an IT context, this is the planning and preparations made to ensure that your organization's technology will still perform in the event of a loss of normal business or technical services.

DR/BC   Disaster recovery/business continuity. Where DR tends to be more IT focused, business continuity is more centered on business users and how they would continue to perform their responsibilities in the event of a disaster.

due diligence   Simply put, are you doing the right thing? Due care is a similar term.

EA   Executive assistant. An individual who supports a senior level executive.

ECTF   Electronic Crimes Task Force. Mandated by the Patriot Act, the U.S. Secret Service was tasked with building regional organizations that included federal, state, and local law enforcement resources, as well as private and academic organizations as part of what it calls an Electronic Crimes Task Force to focus on crimes involving financial services. The ECTF meetings are usually held quarterly in most major U.S. cities.

ERM   Enterprise risk management. With the financial collapse of 2008 and the ensuing devastation to the world economy, many organizations are realizing the need to adequately identify and mitigate the significant risks that face them. Although the original impetus was based on financial risk, ERM has evolved to address all types of risks that face an organization.

FBI   Federal Bureau of Investigation. A governmental agency belonging to the U.S. Department of Justice that investigates federal crimes and also performs the counterintelligence and counter-terrorism functions for the U.S. government.

FFIEC   Federal Financial Institutions Examination Council. A formal interagency body empowered to prescribe uniform principles, standards, and report forms for the federal examination of financial institutions.

field services   Many IT organizations task local IT technicians to respond to and resolve computer issues for end users. These resources are often referred to as field services.

FIRST   Forum of Incident Response and Security Teams. A worldwide organization of computer incident responders and information security professionals.

FTC   Federal Trade Commission. An independent agency of the U.S. government that promotes consumer protection.

FTP   File Transfer Protocol. A standard protocol used to transfer files from one host to another host over the Internet.

GLBA   Gramm Leach Bliley Act, aka the Financial Services Modernization Act of 1999. Obliges financial institutions not only to protect the security and confidentiality of customers' nonpublic personal information, but also for regulators specifically to establish appropriate standards for the financial institutions subject to their jurisdiction relating to administrative, technical, and physical safeguards.

HIDS   Host-based intrusion detection systems. HIDS monitor systems for changes or activities (intrusions) that are malicious and provides alerts.

HIPAA   The Health Insurance Portability and Accountability Act of 1996 requires that healthcare providers, health plans, and healthcare clearinghouses ensure the security and privacy of private health information.

HIPS   Host-based intrusion prevention systems. HIPS monitor systems for changes or activities (intrusions) that are malicious and prevents them from occurring.

HITECH   Health Information Technology for Economic and Clinical Health. A sort of update to HIPAA (*see* HIPAA) that extends the HIPAA requirements to business associates. HITECH also has updated notification requirements in the event of a breach of Personal Health Information (PHI).

HR   Human resources. The business function that manages the organization's employees.

HTTP   HyperText Transfer Protocol. The main technology used for browsing the World Wide Web (www.*.*) .

IAW   In accordance with. A military acronym used to ease writing of orders and plans.

ICC   Incident Control Center. An internal organization that manages production outages and other incidents that disrupt the IT functionality for the organization.

Identity Protection Services   Services provided for a fee that monitor your credit accounts for signs of criminal behavior. These services can also provide support to help you repair your credit should you be a victim of identity theft.

IDS   Intrusion detection system. *See also* HIDS and NIDS. A device or service that typically monitors the environment for signatures of malicious behavior and provides alerts.

IEC   International Electrotechnical Commission. An international standards organization dealing with electrical, electronic, and related technologies.

IM   Instant messaging. The ability to send text messages to others in a real-time fashion not requiring e-mail.

InfoSec   Information security. Protecting information and information systems from unauthorized access, use, disclosure, disruption, modification, or destruction.

InfraGard   An FBI sponsored program encouraging collaboration between the federal government and civilians with responsibility for protecting critical national infrastructure. InfraGard has chapters throughout the United States and typically hosts public meetings on a quarterly basis.

IP   Internet Protocol. An addressing scheme that uniquely identifies entities on the Internet.

IP/MAC address   Internet Protocol/Media Access Control. An addressing scheme that uniquely identifies entities on a physical segment. This physical address (MAC) will typically be linked with a logical (IP) address.

IPS   Intrusion prevention system. *See also* HIPS and NIPS. A device or service that typically monitors the environment for signatures of malicious behavior and blocks or otherwise prevents them from adversely affecting the enterprise.

IR   Incident response. The act of directing resources to mitigate a crisis.

ISACA   Information Systems Audit and Control Association. An international professional association that deals with IT governance.

ISO   In support of. A military acronym used to ease writing of orders and plans.

ISO/IEC 27000   International Organization for Standardization/International Electrotechnical Commission. A published series of standards for information security management systems that is generally acknowledged as one of the best information security frameworks available.

ISO27K   *See* ISO/IEC 27000.

ISSA   Information Systems Security Association is a not-for-profit, international professional organization of Information Security professionals.

IT   Information technology. A branch of engineering that deals with the use of computers and telecommunications to store, retrieve, and transmit information.

ITIL   Information Technology Infrastructure Library. An internationally recognized framework to help companies identify, plan, deliver, and support IT services.

LDAP   Lightweight Directory Access Protocol. An Internet protocol that e-mail and other programs use to look up information from a server.

LE   Law enforcement. Those persons and organizations empowered by law to administer justice.

MA CMR   Massachusetts Code of Massachusetts Rulings. Those laws pertaining to the state of Massachusetts.

malvertisement   An advertisement on the Internet that has been compromised in order to perform some malicious action.

malware   Previously known as viruses; software programs that compromise or otherwise perform some sort of malicious activity on a system without the owner's permission or (often) knowledge.

NC3TF   Northern California Computer Crimes Task Force. A regional task force containing law enforcement personnel from the various police departments and district attorney offices of several Northern California counties for the purpose of working on computer crimes. Members are sworn law enforcement and receive specialized cyber-training as part of their assignment. NC3TF is one of several such organizations within the state of California.

NDA   Non-disclosure agreement. A legal agreement compelling parties not to discuss sensitive information about the other.

NIDS   Network intrusion detection system. *See* IDS.

NIPP   *See* DHS NIPP.

NIPS   Network intrusion prevention system. *See* IPS.

NIST   National Institute of Standards and Technology. Part of the U.S. Department of Commerce, NIST was formerly known as the National Bureau of Standards.

NOC   Network operations center. That organization that manages the use of the organization's networks.

OODA   Observe, orient, decide, act. The four steps of the human cognitive process. Also referred to as the OODA Loop.

PAN   Primary account number. The 16-digit number that is on your credit card.

PCI   Payment Card Industry. A consortium of credit card companies with the purpose of establishing and enforcing a Data Security Standard (DSS) to protect credit card information.

PCI DSS   Payment Card Industry Data Security Standard. The criteria by which organizations are held accountable for the protection of credit card data.

PDAs   Personal digital assistant. Typically some sort of handheld technology that connects the user to the Internet.

PFI   PCI forensic investigator. The new term for what was qualified incident response assessors (QIRA). In the event of a PCI data breach, PFIs may be directed to investigate the data breach. The cost of this involuntary third-party service is typically borne by the compromised organization.

phishing e-mails   Malicious e-mails that surreptitiously cause you to take an action that is to your disadvantage. Often assuming the identity of a trusted source, phishing e-mails lure targeted users into downloading malicious code and/or providing sensitive information under the guise of being a legitimate request.

PII   Personally identifiable information. Information that is typically not available to the public and that is unique to an individual. Various regulations define PII, but there currently is not a consistent legal definition.

PIN   Personal identification number. Typically a series of numbers used to authenticate your identity.

POC   Point of contact. Typically the name and contact information of an individual.

POS   Point of sale. Technology used to process credit and debit cards as a form of payment for goods/services rendered.

QIRA   Qualified incident response assessors. Currently called PCI forensic investigators (PFI). *See* PFI.

R&D   Research & Development. Work directed toward the innovation, introduction, and improvement of products and processes.

REACT   Rapid Enforcement Allied Computer Team. An awkward acronym for Silicon Valley's regional computer crimes task force. *See* NC3TF.

SB-24   *See* CA SB-24.

Secret Service   The U.S. Secret Service, part of the Department of Homeland Security, is primarily tasked with protecting the President of the United States and other key political figures. Their secondary duty was investigating counterfeit U.S. currency. Their responsibilities expanded to safeguarding the nation's financial infrastructure and payment systems including online credit card crimes. For additional information, *see* ECTF.

SIG   Special interest group. A collection of people with a shared interest.

signature-based technology   An industry approach that bases its preventative and detective capabilities on signatures, or recognizable patterns, of known threats/attacks.

SME   Subject matter expert. An individual with superior expertise in a specific topic or technology.

SMTP   Simple Mail Transfer Protocol. The standard for sending e-mail via the Internet.

SOC   Service organization controls. Audit reports that provide an independent verification of the validity of an organizations security controls. Typically referred to as SOC-1, SOC-2, and SOC-3 reports.

SOP   Standard operating procedure. A documented process uniformly applied to an organization.

SOW   Scope of work. A detailed description of the work to be provided by a third-party contractor, consultant, or firm.

SOX   The Sarbanes-Oxley Act. A Federal law that requires companies to report on the effectiveness of their internal controls.

spear-phishing   E-mail phishing (*see* phishing e-mail) directed at a more deliberate target audience in order to improve the success rate of a phishing attack. Another term, "whaling," is also used to describe a spear-phishing attack against the really "big fish" of an organization (such as a CEO).

SYSLOG   Systems logging. The process of accumulating records of events pertaining to a specific IT device or service for the purpose of audit, forensic and monitoring functions

TSA   Transportation Security Administration. A federal agency developed to safeguard the transportation systems of the United States.

US CERT GFIRST   United States Computer Emergency Response Team Government Forum of Incident Responders and Security Teams. An annual computer security conference hosted by the U.S. Department of Homeland Security. Although primarily focused on government organizations, I have found this event to be well worth the effort. The FBI-sponsored InfraGard program typically conducts its annual national meeting in conjunction with the GFIRST conference.

US DHS   United States Department of Homeland Security. *See* Department of Homeland Security above.

USSS   United States Secret Service. *See* Secret Service above.

zero-day, zero-day exploit   An unknown cyber threat for which the InfoSec industry (*see* signature-based technology) has not had sufficient time or knowledge to adequately detect or prevent.

Index

Stop Hackers in Their Tracks

Hacking Exposed, 7th Edition

Hacking Exposed
Malware & Rootkits

Hacking Exposed Computer
Forensics, 2nd Edition

Hacking Exposed Wireless,
2nd Edition

Hacking Exposed:
Web Applications, 3rd Edition

Hacking Exposed Linux,
3rd Edition

IT Auditing,
2nd Edition

IT Security Metrics

Gray Hat Hacking,
2nd Edition